H A U N T

SOME

MONSTERS

ARE

REAL

HAUNT

SCREENPLAY & FILMMAKER DIARIES

Scott Beck & Bryan Woods

Published by Bold Words
Los Angeles, California

First Printing, October 2022

ISBN: 979-8-218-05913-2

BOLD/WORDS

CONTENTS

INTRODUCTION

Making a movie is exhilarating. And horrifying! It makes you feel wonderful. And depressed!

After working professionally in the film business for over a decade, it's become painfully clear to us that there are only high-highs and low-lows, no safe comforting in-betweens, which makes this profession an emotional rollercoaster that we find occasionally difficult to cope with. So we started keeping a journal. Recording every little stumble and every big fall. It's therapy. When your movie falls apart, or a studio rejects your script, or the audience tells you how much you suck, it seems to hurt a little less knowing that one day those experiences will be a small blurb in a diary that you can laugh about with your friends. Or in this case with you.

The following pages contain excerpts from each of our journals during the making of *Haunt*, written separately but collated and edited for a streamlined experience. In a few areas names of people, projects, and companies have been changed or redacted to protect relationships and future endeavors. But we did our best to preserve the truth of our experiences, no matter how embarrassing it is for us (which it often is), because that's the point of a project like this.

There are better filmmakers who have written better journals that we encourage you to explore: Steven Soderbergh's "Getting Away With It", Robert Rodriguez's "Roadracers: the Making of a Degenerate Hot Rod Flick", and Tom DiCillo's "Box of Moonlight & Notes from Overboard", to name only a few. It is in the tradition of those books that we have assembled our own. And our humble dream is that every filmmaker who reads this book considers keeping their own journal, and one day shares it with us too.

Beck/Woods
Los Angeles, California
October 2022

FILMMAKER DIARIES

TUESDAY, AUGUST 23RD 2016 **(Beck)**

Yesterday was a weird day. Point of proof, is that the last two missed calls and voicemails I received were from Paramount Pictures and William Morris Endeavor. Turns out Paramount is making an offer on *A Quiet Place* this week. Super surreal, and I'm both parts excited and skeptical about this upcoming process. I mean, we wrote the movie to produce on the cheap (like $60-100k) and now we could be talking about full-fledged studio backing – on a 67-page spec script with hardly any dialogue. But what are the studio notes going to look like? Will they want more dialogue in the film, thus deflating the entire concept? Or will they want more creatures? Really hope we don't sell our soul... but it's Paramount!

Crazy coincidence is that the VP who read and passed the script up the ladder is Alana Mayo, who was the very first general meeting we ever had in LA six years ago, after she had screened our short film *Impulse*.[1] As I get older, I'm realizing how much smaller Hollywood seems to get.

Nice to get news like this, since yesterday we were banging our heads against the wall after reading our first full pass on *Haunt* and were feeling defeated.

Recently Watched: *Parade ('74), Playtime, Star Trek Beyond, The Bad News Bears ('76), Airplane!*

TUESDAY, AUGUST 30TH 2016 **(Beck)**

Sent in the latest pass of our untitled haunted Airport movie - lol.

This thing has been a year in the making, and all we have to show for our thousand hours of work is a terrible 20-page treatment.

Damien Chazelle is getting write-ups about his upcoming film, *La La Land*. Super excited to see it. Wonder how he balanced his passion

---

[1] *Impulse* is a post-apocalyptic short film we wrote and directed in 2009. Featuring only a couple lines of dialogue, the film was a precursor to our concept for *A Quiet Place*.

projects (*Whiplash*, etc.) with his writing assignments (*Grand Piano, Last Exorcism II*). Now he must have carte blanche.

Recently Watched: *The Texas Chain Saw Massacre ('74), The Underneath ('95), The Nice Guys, Overnight, The Rock, Weiner*

WEDNESDAY, SEPTEMBER 7TH 2016 **(Woods)**
Reading Soderbergh's *Sex, Lies, and Videotape* diary book. It's incredible. Half script, half journal of making the movie. Maybe we should try something like that someday?

Recently Watched: *Twin Peaks, The Dark Knight, Side Effects*

TUESDAY, SEPTEMBER 13TH 2016 **(Beck)**
Realized I skipped my entry last week unintentionally and, for the life of me, can't think of what I was specifically working on seven days ago. I do remember that we turned in the first draft of *Haunt* to our producers last Friday, and now awaiting their first notes. We're also still waiting on the offer for *A Quiet Place*. And our pitch for *Layover* finally (finally finally) got sent into Mythology Entertainment, but we're waiting on notes. And – good news – we sold our pilot pitch for *Hero* to MTV (aka we'll be hired to write it), but we're waiting on the network's feedback before marching ahead. Soooo Bryan and I are in a bit of a standstill and I feel super guilty when idle. Of course we could always find our own ways to be proactive, like forging ahead on past projects, but I can also find lots of ways to waste time on the internet. Yesterday I spent almost the entire day working on a dumb video for Bryan's birthday, which is tomorrow. So yes, I feel like a piece of shit and need to get back to real work.

Recently Watched: *Hell or High Water, The Kid Stays in the Picture, Magic in the Moonlight, Jour de Fête, 25ᵗʰ Hour, Unfaithfully Yours*

THURSDAY, SEPTEMBER 22ND 2016 **(Beck)**
Finally heard back from Paramount and we've closed the *A Quiet Place* deal. Apparently Michael Bay was having dinner with studio president Marc Evans on Monday night and told him to get the deal

done. Don't know if that's just fluff from our agents or if it's totally legit, but I'm choosing the latter... after all, I need to latch on to some fun script sale narrative. We're having our first meeting at the studio next Tuesday to discuss what the next steps are, and I'm simultaneously excited and bracing myself for a shitstorm of notes.

Hitting up the Michael Giacchino *Lost* concert tonight. My cinematic soul always gets refilled listening to my favorite composers. Wish he would take a request and play some of his *Speed Racer* or *Super 8* score.

Recently Watched: *Ocean's Twelve, Snowden, The Bride Wore Black, Ocean's Thirteen, Chained*

WEDNESDAY, OCTOBER 12ᵀᴴ 2016 **(Woods)**

Racing through rewrites for *A Quiet Place*. This project seems to have real momentum. Though the studio notes made us sweat a bit.

To:
From:
Subject: A QUIET PLACE —
Date: 9.26.16

We're so excited to be working with all of you on this one! The family dynamic at the heart of this story is so compelling and we love the suspense and pervasive tension that spans every scene of the film. As you continue work on the draft, it would be great to look for ways to make this story and setting feel as singular and distinct as possible. Key to that is finding ways to provide more context as to the state of the world, how the alien invasion began and what this family's place is within that greater context. For instance, would be great to get a better understanding of how the aliens terrorizing this family ended up on Earth and what has happened to the rest of the country and the world since it has arrived.

They really wanted us to unpack the mythology of the aliens and explain more about the outside world. We've always felt this story should be an intimate experience completely focused on this one family.

After a few weeks of work, we think we've come up with some subtle solutions that hint at the outside world without breaking the film's unique point of view, and actually makes the script stronger. Bloated this sucker up from 67 pages to 85. Seeing the Paramount letterhead on the notes doc is pretty much the highlight of our career.

Recently Watched: *A Face in the Crowd ('57), 12 Angry Men ('57), All the President's Men*

TUESDAY, NOVEMBER 23RD 2016 **(Beck)**

Off to Iowa for Thanksgiving. Was originally supposed to hand in a draft of our TV pilot *Hero* to our producers before the break. But come on, that was a 3 week turnaround time and I'm slower than Gus Van Sant's *Gerry* (which, don't get me wrong, I adore). I only just finished Act Two (out of Five) yesterday, which means I might be cramming my life with more than turkey over the break.

Recently Watched: *Gambler ('06), Swiss Army Man, American Movie, Nocturnal Animals, Notorious ('46), The Last Waltz ('78)*

TUESDAY, JANUARY 10TH 2017 **(Woods)**

Delivering *Hero* revisions today. Both Scott and I feel like we didn't make dramatic enough changes. Especially since the first words out of our producer's mouth was "This is a great start" which is code for "Not so fucking great, hotshot! Time to rip some stuff up!". Well, we didn't. We just took what we loved, modified it, strengthened it, and then tossed in some throwaway lines that were VERY on the nose to satisfy the problems everyone brought up. Not a great way to be a working screenwriter in this town. But Scott and I often have trouble with revising something if we don't share the problem. In this case, a lot of what our producer was saying we understood and agreed with, but the solutions they presented would require abandoning stuff that we think is strong, and ultimately would create a bigger problem than the one we're trying to solve.

Recently Watched: *La La Land, Knight of Cups, Twin Peaks*

WEDNESDAY, JANUARY 11TH 2017 **(Woods)**

Such a packed day. Had a meeting about *Haunt* at Broken Road that went terrific.[2] It's the first time we've walked out of there with big smiles on our faces. Everyone is excited to move forward making this movie. The casting talks were brief, and preliminary, but I was happy they've backed off the social media influencer angle. We are being given a little license to find strong up-and-comers that we're excited about. Scott and I are putting together our cast list and will share with Broken Road tomorrow.

Closed the day by getting an email from our agent saying John Davis would love for us to crack a *Chronicle 2* take, and that he's very excited about our new TV pilot. Anyway, *Chronicle* is a damn near masterpiece and we're not gonna come up with something better.

Recently Watched: *It Follows, Mulholland Drive*

THURSDAY, JANUARY 12TH 2017 (Woods)

Just got back from a meeting with Dan Cohen at 21 Laps. Holy shit have they had a great year… *Arrival* and *Stranger Things*. Embarrassed myself several times by gushing, since those were my two favorite narrative experiences in each medium this year. Dan was an early champion of our *Nightlight* script.[3] We pitched him the short story of "Needle in a Timestack" by Robert Silverberg, which he loved and immediately got on the phone to track down the rights.[4] Seems Miramax still has it. But is it in active development? Or has it been dormant for years? Dan is going to do more digging, and in the meantime will send him a few other articles/stories that have captured our imagination. Dan also mentioned he'd be interested in getting us staffed on *Stranger Things*, but we think we'd be terrible staff writers.

---

[2] Broken Road Productions is run by veteran producer Todd Garner, along with his team Sean Robins and Jeremy Stein. They are best known for *Mortal Kombat, Isn't It Romantic, Tag*, and of course, *Haunt*.

[3] The spec script for *Nightlight* was our first professional sale. We later directed the movie, which was released by Lionsgate on March 27th, 2015.

[4] Not one month after we reached out about this project, the dormant film was suddenly fast-tracked. A year later we found ourselves in a surreal meeting with Orlando Bloom as he told us about a movie he just completed with writer/director John Ridley. That film, *Needle in a Timestack*, was eventually released October 15th, 2021.

FRIDAY, JANUARY 13ᵀᴴ 2017 (Woods)

Had a meeting with our manager Ryan at Madhouse to discuss 2017 goals. He is excited about what this year could bring, and wants to make sure we're managing our time appropriately. Day ended with a call from the producers on our TV pilot *Hero*. Think they saw through our bullshit attempts at giving the pilot narrative thrust. They pitched another angle on the opening to get people excited and dialed in, but honestly, just think it will end up making everything worse. We'll give it a try over the weekend. Producers are pretty sure the network is gonna be like "wtf is this? 22 pages of nothing happening, where is this going?" and I'm sure they're right. But we don't want the pilot to suck, either.

Bought an Xbox today to… cope.

Recently Watched: *Sex, Lies, and Videotape, The Sea of Trees, Harry Potter and the Sorcerer's Stone, Harry Potter and the Chamber of Secrets, Harry Potter and the Prisoner of Azkaban, The Path (Season 1)*

WEDNESDAY, JANUARY 18ᵀᴴ 2017 (Woods)

Call from Dan Cohen 21 LAPS re: *Needle in a Timestack*:

"I'm trying to get specifics… still tied up at Miramax… they have a writer… but he's trying to get specific about what's going on… so maybe we could all produce…?"

We told him about our love of the Stephen King short story "The Boogeyman" and how we'd love to do it as a feature. He said:

"*Boogeyman*, let's just do that – it would be great, I'm very familiar with the story… if it's avail let's do it."

Recently Watched: *Ides of March, Don't Think Twice, The TV Set, Shut Eye (Pilot), Ouija: Origin of Evil, The TV Set (w/commentary)*

WEDNESDAY, JANUARY 25ᵀᴴ 2017 (Woods)

Yesterday was a full day of meetings. Met with Atlas Entertainment in the morning. We accidentally left their office through the service elevator, then zig-zagged back to the lobby, only for a very cordial Billy Bob Thornton to hold the door for us. Then had lunch with Milo Ventimiglia (who is star of the biggest show of the moment *This Is Us*) and his producing partner Russ Cundiff. They are great guys, with a blue-collar work ethic vibe that we really connected with. Left that for Red Studios, where we reconnected with Sarah Esberg over at Plan B. Scott went into an unprompted pitch for one of our favorite horror ideas, and we later realized that we had already pitched that idea to her two years ago. So they had to pass twice. Oops. Anyway, Sarah's the best – has a cool poster for *Don't Look Now* on her wall.

Recently Watched: *O.J. Simpson: Made in America, Where to Invade Next, The Edge of Seventeen, The Founder*

SATURDAY, JANUARY 28TH 2017 (Woods)

Met with Scott Strauss at Screen Gems. It has been a dream of ours for the longest time to reboot the *Resident Evil* franchise, not as a hokey over the top action movie, but as a Gus Van Sant long walk into dread. The *Batman Begins* version so to speak. For a moment, late into the meeting, it suddenly felt like our entire career had been building up to Scott telling us that they were indeed looking into rebooting the franchise. And what's more, they wanted to do it at a $5 million dollar price, and find young up-and-comers like ourselves to work on it. My god. All of the planets have finally aligned. We left the meeting on Cloud 9 and urgently called our manager to tell him: drop everything, let Screen Gems know we're coming in next week with a *Resident Evil* pitch. Before we could even properly convey our enthusiasm, our manager informed us there's already another writer doing the movie for James Wan's Atomic Monster. Waaaaaaaaaaah-Waaaaaaaaaaaaaaahh. Our spirits deflated immediately.

Recently Watched: *Nocturnal Animals, The Social Network, iBoy, Split, The Limey*

WEDNESDAY, FEBRUARY 7TH 2017 (Beck)

Fascinating turn of events with *Haunt*. It all started with a Screen Gems meeting last week, in which we pitched the script to the head.

He read and dug it, and passed it along to his boss (still waiting on his response), with the possibility their studio might come on board and make this a much larger film. So we get a call this morning from Broken Road, and our producer Jeremy says he has "good news". I'm expecting to hear that Screen Gems wants in, but instead he says Eli Roth read the script last night and flipped for it. Supposedly he's been trying to crack a haunted house idea for a while but has never found a solid execution. Now he wants to come on board.

Got a small round of notes on *Hero* from Sony. Everyone's excited! About to knock these out and turn a draft around in a day, which will finally go into MTV.

Recently Watched: *Bound for Glory, Bubble, Live By Night, The Wages of Fear, Shine a Light*

WEDNESDAY, FEBRUARY 9TH 2017 (Beck)
So news broke today that the head of MTV left for Facebook and the CEO of Viacom simultaneously announced that he's completely changing the network's mandate – more reality shows, more Viacom-owned IP, less scripted series. What does this mean? We don't have our network executive anymore. And because of the new mandate, we're being told that it is 99% likely that MTV will be passing on our pilot before they even read it. Which is ironic, considering we just turned in the network draft <u>TONIGHT</u>.

WEDNESDAY, FEBRUARY 22ND 2017 (Beck)
Last Monday, we met with Eli Roth. He was deep in an edit on his upcoming *Death Wish* remake (saw some awesome footage – Bruce gets payback on a guy in an autobody shop). Eli was great. He totally got the vision for *Haunt*, even referenced our biggest touchstone *Green Room* before we had a chance to bring it up. He digs and more so supports the idea of casting normal, relatable-looking actors, and challenged us to ground the horror and figure out the mythology in the same way that Tarantino challenged him on *Hostel*.

Bottomline, Eli is on board. Which means we're going into distributors (MGM, Screen Gems, Stage 6, etc.) with this new package and rewrites (which we tackled this last week) and see if we can get bites. We also just heard the budget is increasing either 200 or 300 percent which would really help us make a better movie.

And then, also last week, we got an email from our manager asking if we've seen any of Netflix's series *The OA,* and if we'd consider staffing on it. Of course our answer was an emphatic YES. It's one of the most beautifully crafted stories ever made. We met the show creators, Brit & Zal, and we got along so fucking well. Ended up talking for two hours in their new writers room (aka a house in Silver Lake), and ended the meeting with some mystic conversation of happenstance in which I was talking about Alexander Payne, who in a roundabout way connected us to our first producer who packaged our first feature with Payne's producer Michael London. Zal got this shocked look on his face and said Payne lives downstairs. I don't believe in fate or cosmic connections, but this meeting made me second guess. Brit & Zal were so fucking cool.

Recently Watched: *Fargo, Broadcast News, Black Sunday*

WEDNESDAY, MARCH 8TH 2017 (Woods)
So much has happened since last writing, where to begin…? Netflix officially offered us *The OA* and we may have to gracefully bow out because we're overbooked.

Eli Roth is encouraging us to make the *Haunt* characters stronger. He has intelligent, energetic notes. It's been surprisingly hard opening the script up for the hundredth time, revising the characters up top and trying to get them to back into everything that follows in act 2 and 3. I often wonder if we are just making these characters worse, or focusing precious real estate on characters who are less important at the expense of characters who matter.

The *A Quiet Place* casting breakdown went out this week, things are gearing up.

Our MTV pilot *Hero* is officially dead, but now that we have a script there's talk of reintroducing it to the marketplace in hopes of landing a different network.

And finally, I watched *Murder à la Mod,* one of Brian De Palma's first features (the first he both wrote and directed) – it's a horror comedy, that was kind of universally dismissed…. Negative reviews, etc etc. I really feel a kinship with De Palma because he's incredibly visual as a filmmaker (sometimes at the expense of story). The aesthetic choices he makes are the aesthetic choices I love. And even though some of his films are personal… he seems to need a film or filmmaker as a jumping off point for inspiration, like the magnifying glass he typically hovers over Hitchcock.

Recently Watched: *Murder à la Mod, Dazed and Confused, Knock Knock, Billy Madison, Cursed, Girls (Season 4)*

MONDAY, MARCH 13TH 2017 **(Woods)**

Turned down *The OA* today… I feel… sad? Yeah, that's sadness.

Recently Watched: *Rosemary's Baby, Big Little Lies, Crashing, Girls (Season 4), Everybody Wants Some!!*

WEDNESDAY, MARCH 15TH 2017 **(Woods)**

Press release for *A Quiet Place* dropped today and we weren't mentioned.

Writers are usually ignored in this business, so it's not a surprise, but we're still pretty disappointed.

Eli Roth approved our new draft of *Haunt.* Don't know if he genuinely loved the new changes, or just wanted to keep up the

John Krasinski to Write, Direct and Star With Emily Blunt in 'Quiet' Thriller

By Justin Kroll

momentum, but regardless he sent us a lovely email – and the script went out to a few places over the weekend for potential partnerships. Haven't heard anything yet, so not sure if that means people are... passing?... but our producers promise us the movie will go forward regardless if another financier comes in. Scott and I are very skeptical about that. But I hope the train keeps moving – because we're desperate to get back into the director's chair. If it doesn't work out... well... we still have the blind deal with Paramount (which we just closed), and 21 Laps is all set for our *Boogeyman*/Stephen King project.[5]

Recently Watched: *The Girl on the Train, Logan, Girls (Season 4)*

THURSDAY, MARCH 30TH 2017 (Woods)

Julia and I went to *The Discovery* premiere last night, held at the greatest theater in possibly the world, The Vista. Right away it was like... oh there's Ted Danson, there's Jason Segel, Mary Steenburgen, and on and on. I don't really get starstruck, but it's fun to see some familiar faces.

Charlie McDowell's film was somber, intriguing, atmospheric, in places brilliantly performed (with a scene stealing supporting turn by Jesse Plemons). Funny and original, *The Discovery* is a movie that should be seen, and I'm grateful I got to be part of the premiere thanks to Julia who logged countless hours as an assistant to the producers. Really proud of her and the entire team.

At the after party, I started getting insane anxiety. I was sort of dreading it all night. Loud bars where people are drinking just aren't my scene. Especially when I don't know anyone, and it's just a bunch of Hollywood dbags stumbling around talking about the famous/cool/talented people they know. That's too harsh. Mostly wonderful people there. I assume! Really, I just get scared and shy,

---

[5] Paramount's enthusiasm for the *A Quiet Place* spec script was so strong, they offered us what's known as a "blind deal", i.e., a pre-negotiated deal to buy our next writing/directing project before we've even come up with it.

and for some reason last night could not fake any enthusiasm at all. Julia could tell right away that I was in over my head. Especially after a few awkward exchanges with her friends in which I contributed nothing and just had a sad, bored look on my face. I pulled her aside, apologized, my anxiety building the more I realized I'm ruining her big night and this isn't about me. But luckily she let me off the hook, said she understood. We agreed to step outside into the porch area to get a breath of fresh air and chill. We go outside, sit down, and who do we see sitting right there, avoiding the bullshit like us....???

Edgar Wright and David Fincher. When I said earlier that I don't get "starstruck"... that was a big fucking lie. Holy shit, two giants of cinema. One of whom we quote endlessly. Julia has a post-it note on her computer that says "Be Zen Like Fincher" – it's a mantra we repeat often to ourselves, because Fincher seems so relaxed on behind the scenes segments and interviews. It's like he doesn't let all the bullshit get to him. He just perseveres. I snapped a stalkery low-light picture to prove I wasn't imagining things, located below.

David Fincher (left) and Edgar Wright at *The Discovery* after party.

Recently Watched: *Elle, Project Almanac, Everybody Wants Some!!, Girls (Season 5), Beauty and the Beast, The Discovery, Girls (Season 6), Big Little Lies, Crashing*

THURSDAY, APRIL 20TH 2017 **(Woods)**

Lunch with John Graham and Jessica Switch of Studio 8 yesterday. Lots of fun catching up with those two. Also met our agent's brother Matt Cohan who works at Bay Films for the maestro Michael Bay himself. Said they've heard Paramount is super hyped on *A Quiet Place*, they're saying "it's one of the best scripts of the last five years".

21 Laps is calling every other day. Had a great *Boogeyman* meeting with them last week – they along with Madhouse are producing the project. They've officially optioned the Stephen King short, and we have 6 months to set it up at a studio.

Haunt has been eerily silent for a couple weeks now. Ryan checked our avail with our producer Mark Fasano at Nickel City (in case we might want to reassess the Netflix gig) and it sounds like there's interest from Sierra/Affinity, Lionsgate, 2929, Dimension, and Bron Films, so stay tuned to find out if any of this pans out. Why aren't we on set already???? Hurry up and... wait.

Recently Watched: *Dogville, Close Encounters of the Third Kind, Baskets, Girls, Utopia, Steve Jobs, Mr. Right, 20th Century Women, The Great Gatsby (Luhrman), The Bad News Bears (Linklater), Life*

SATURDAY, APRIL 22ND 2017 **(Woods)**

Lovely weekend with Julia at THE FESTIVAL OF BOOKS in downtown LA. Saw Sherry Lansing speak.[6] Tears in my eyes the whole time. Such an inspiring figure. Other highlights included Margaret Atwood, Michael Ovitz (Julia's favorite panel), Joyce Carol Oates, and the food trucks, let's not forget the greasy burgers and hot dogs for me, and the exotic food for Jubie. Julia and I are awful at getting books signed. We feel awkward, don't know what to say, don't know the proper protocol.

Recently Watched: *Lord of the Rings: The Fellowship of the Ring (Extended Cut), Suicide Squad, Baskets, The Lost City of Z*

---

[6] Sherry Lansing was the CEO of Paramount Pictures from 1992 to 2005.

TUESDAY, APRIL 25TH 2017 **(Woods)**

Scott and I were talking about how we've both psychologically moved on from *Haunt*, because it's been radio silence for what feels like a month now, and there's no point in dwelling on a project that might be dead, and not two hours later we get a call from Jeremy Stein saying Sierra/Affinity wants to move forward with the project.[7] SO COOL. I don't know, this business is so weird and gratifying, sometimes you almost forget how depressing it all is.

Recently Watched: *Elysium, Shoot the Piano Player, Inside Man*

SUNDAY, APRIL 30TH 2017 **(Woods)**

Holy shit, Scott and Christy are having a baby!!! Couldn't be happier, more proud, etc etc. They will make truly terrific parents! I've been waiting for this moment for a long time. Why did it take them so long??? Odd night for us all to watch *Borat*.

Recently Watched: *Borat, The Prestige, An Honest Liar, War Dogs, Cabin Fever, American Honey*

TUESDAY, MAY 2ND 2017 **(Woods)**

Had our meeting with Sierra today. The Master of Terror Eli Roth made a big speech about how he wants to independently own the movie and monsters, that *Haunt* has the potential to be a franchise. And how he wants to premiere at Toronto Midnight, and after the movie finishes playing, make all the buyers leave the theater and walk into a haunted house that's filled with the monsters from our movie. It's a great idea and why I'm so thankful Eli and Todd are producing this project.

Sierra responded to the pitch well enough, but by no means seemed ready to write a check. So much for Mark's email "SIERRA WANTS TO MOVE FORWARD!!" Scott did a great job of following up the Eli/Todd hype train by communicating our vision and enthusiasm for

---

[7] Sierra/Affinity is a leading film finance, production and international sales company.

our story. I was a bit DOA today, not quite on my A-game unfortunately. But I contributed just enough to not embarrass myself. Scott left the meeting feeling pretty positive, like Sierra might actually come on board, despite agreeing it's by no means a sure thing. But I'm not convinced at all. Honestly, felt like a polite pass to me. Everyone was good natured and non-committal enough that they could easily walk away and no harm would be done.

Recently Watched: *Children of Men, Solaris ('02), Silicon Valley*

THURSDAY, MAY 4ᵀᴴ 2017 (Woods)

So I was dead wrong about Sierra. Got an email from Mark and it sounds like they are ready to come aboard *Haunt*. They have some notes about the first act (cue instant ball of stress in my gut), but are excited to make a non-cast contingent movie in Canada with us and Eli. Very fucking stoked for next steps. But also very nervous. Both *A Quiet Place* and *Haunt* will probably be filming at the same time.

21 Laps asked for our rewrite quote today and have set a meeting for us and Joseph Gordon-Levitt on the sci-fi project *Station* (back to Sierra/Affinity we go!). I have no idea how we'll have time for this rewrite in the face of prepping/rewriting *Haunt*, pitching on our blind, prepping pitch for *Boogeyman* (option expires in less than 6 months), and everything else we have going on. It's an embarrassment of riches and we are grateful. Man, exactly one year ago things were sooo fucking dire. It seemed like no one wanted to make a movie with us and we weren't passionate about anything we were working on.

Recently Watched: *The Vanishing ('88), Slacker, Victor Frankenstein*

FRIDAY, MAY 5ᵀᴴ 2017 (Woods)

Saw two underrated Scorsese classics at the Aero with Julia for their Michael Ballhaus tribute. *After Hours* is my favorite of their collaborations. Watched it out of obligation in college because it was included in a Scorsese DVD boxset I owned. After the explosive opening shot and subsequent fifteen minutes, I placed the film on pause, went upstairs, and promptly started making popcorn, knowing that I was about to have one of the best cinematic experiences of my life. The remainder of the film did not disappoint. Seeing it in LA on the big screen, with my girlfriend, and a very enthusiastic audience, was such a beautiful, hilarious, and heartwarming experience.

Manager called late Friday with a weird proposition. ███████████ is producing the ███████████████ movie for ██████████.[8] The studio asked if we'd be willing to read the script over the weekend (just the first two acts) and come up with an ending. What a hilarious way to go about a writing "bake off". Fortunately we don't really have time for this bullshit.

Recently Watched: *Cabin Fever, After Hours, The Color of Money, Comet, The Mick*

TUESDAY, MAY 9TH 2017 **(Woods)**
Got the financier's notes on *Haunt*. They came in much bigger than originally pitched. This always happens. Everyone always lures you in with "we only have a couple thoughts" and then as soon as they have you "oops, I guess there were a few more notes than we thought." The notes are smart. We can vaguely understand where most are coming from, though one calls for a near page one rewrite of Act 1, which is unfortunate. We're in the process of pushing back a little bit to see how much leash they're giving us, and also challenging a few of their notes that might weaken the script in ways they don't anticipate. Whenever you work with someone new, particularly a studio or financier, you never know how much you can push back before you're considered difficult to work with.

Recently Watched: *Arrival, Viral, Get Out*

TUESDAY, JUNE 6TH 2017 **(Woods)**
Our TV pilot *Hero* is going out to networks. It's into Freeform, Netflix, USA/SyFy, CW, FBC, TNT, and Amazon.

---

[8] This project was based on very high-profile intellectual property. The resulting film was a critical and financial disappointment.

The exciting news came with the disappointing reveal that YouTube already passed. Doesn't matter how much good news you get, when someone passes on something you're proud of, it always hurts. Immediately a fog descends upon you, souring your mood, and clouding your creativity. Since Sony pre-emptively slipped the pilot to YouTube, we assume that was our best shot. Had also heard YouTube was looking for stuff exactly like this – young, cool, edgy, with young leads. Afraid this pass could be a whisper of things to come.

Recently Watched: *National Treasure (miniseries), Hail, Caesar!, 21 Years: Richard Linklater, The Last Action Hero*

WEDNESDAY, JUNE 14TH 2017 (Woods)
Last night we received a congratulatory email from Josie at Sierra saying they finally closed their *Haunt* deal; she wants to take us to lunch. Cool!

FIVE MINUTES LATER –

Oh, our TV producer is calling... he says good news/bad news on the *Hero* front. Good news, script is amazing. Bad news, there are soooo many superhero shows right now. We have to convince networks that this is better than what they already bought, or different than what's already on TV.

Our producer says he's been in this place before, and the only thing you can do is get the material in the best shape possible so that it speaks for itself, which he believes we have accomplished. But he wants us to be realistic about prospects. This actually sounds like bad news/worse news.

Recently Watched: *The Village, 12 Monkeys, The Hamster Factor (Making of 12 Monkeys), Get Out, Silicon Valley, Master of None*

FRIDAY, JUNE 16TH 2017 (Woods)
Haunt has a start date... October 16th, 2017. I can think of very few things in life that would be more fun than making a scary movie in

the month of Halloween.

WEDNESDAY, JUNE 28TH 2017 **(Woods)**

Going into Sierra today to discuss our re-writes. Seems they have the exact same two notes as before and are unwilling to compromise. I have lots to say on this, but I jammed my thumb last night at our championship soccer game, and am having difficulty typing. Had to wear sweatpants today because I couldn't button up my jeans. We lost, by the way. Am currently preparing for this Sierra meeting.

So much of this job is salesmanship and arguing. It's really like being a lawyer, except the pay sucks.

Recently Watched: *Split, The Village, Silicon Valley*

THURSDAY, JUNE 29TH 2017 **(Woods)**

The Sierra meeting was a battle, but ultimately everyone heard each other out.

Mostly keep this journal for film stuff, but on a brief personal note: I think about proposing to Julia a lot. I vaguely know how I'm going to do it. Just don't know when. I think being single my whole life has made this process more daunting than it needs to be.

Recently Watched: *What Lies Beneath*

WEDNESDAY, JULY 5TH 2017 **(Woods)**

Worried this journal has become an excuse to procrastinate from re-write work I'm unmotivated to accomplish. Press release for *Haunt* is supposed to drop this week. It's always fun anticipating a trade announcement. It's like this secret we've been sitting on for over a year and now we finally get to brag to our families about it.

A24 remains interested in our indie script *River* as a Forager co-production.[9] But it's pretty low on the totem pole over there and would need a hard sell to the top brass to have a chance (maybe it's a

---

[9] *River* is a script we wrote in college and still hope to make someday.

fit for the blind deal?). I was watching the special features on my new Arrow Video Blu-ray *The Bird with the Crystal Plumage*, and Dario Argento was talking about how the financiers watched the rough cut of his film and immediately decided it was a failure. Too weird, not scary, etc. Meanwhile the producer (Argento's father) heads into the lobby and notices the secretary's hands shaking. He asked if everything was alright, and she responded, "That movie really disturbed me." The producer pleaded with the financiers to give the film a proper release, explaining how the secretary was indicative of their future audience. The film was a failure in the first two cities it opened in. But it finally got traction in Rome, where audience word of mouth fueled it into a big success, with people applauding at the end of every screening. The financiers of course took credit for it and "knew it would be a hit all along". Just goes to show it doesn't matter what country you're making movies in, the money people always know what's best, especially when they don't.

Recently Watched: *Power Rangers, The Beguiled, The Big Sick, Interstellar, Baby Driver, The Bird with the Crystal Plumage, Mimic*

THURSDAY, JULY 6TH 2017 (Woods)

All I want to do is write our project 65 movie. It's so far away from happening with all the stuff on our plate. Good problem to have. Had a meeting at Bruckheimer Films this morning. We were waiting in the lobby and a clean cut, tall man with a slender frame, walks in. I hear Scott say, "Excuse me sir, are you Joseph Kosinski?" Joseph is not only a terrific director (*Tron: Legacy, Oblivion*) whom Scott and I admire, but he also happens to be one of the very, very, very few superstar Hollywood directors from our home state of Iowa. He was generous with his time, sat down next to us, and talked Happy Joe's pizza and Rudy's Tacos for a moment. And then he was whisked away by the man himself, Jerry Bruckheimer, who has commissioned Joseph to direct TOP GUN 2.[10] Actually it was kind of a who's who

---

[10] As of the publishing of this book, both "project 65" aka *65*, and "Top Gun 2" aka *Maverick*, will be released in theaters nearly five years after this chance encounter.

of Hollywood there. Chris Hemsworth was strolling around having just seen a rough cut of his new film with Bruckheimer. And then Craig Mazin (of Scriptnotes Podcast fame) sat down next to us waiting for a meeting. Couldn't help but notice when people reach the upper echelon of Hollywood like all these folks, they don't have to wait very long for their meeting to start. For us nobodies, on the other hand, it's not uncommon to wait 30 minutes to get the call.

Amazon passed on our TV pilot. Hell, <u>everyone</u> has passed on our TV pilot by now. Heard they loved it but characters are too young. This is a common theme in our career.

Recently Watched: *Plastic Galaxy: The Story of Star Wars Toys*

TUESDAY, JULY 11TH 2017 (Woods)

Someone died in our apartment pool last night. I think his name was Louis. He was swimming laps and then sunk to the bottom of the deep end. My neighbors tried to resuscitate him. I arrived home moments after this all happened.

Louis was a really nice, fun, gregarious guy. Loud, very loud. Pretty sure the entire apartment complex got to know him through his voice, which would echo around the walls of the pool area when he was on the phone. I had the pleasure of talking to him a few times – even as recently as a couple days ago, when I saw him fall off his bike. I stopped to make sure he was okay and noticed he had a Zog Sports shirt on. Told him I was familiar with the league and asked if he played any sports. He said he used to play football with Zog, and that he'd like to get back into doing it again. "A lot of running though," he said. A funny comment from someone who was in such good shape.

It became clear in the past several months that Louis was struggling with some form of drug or alcohol addiction. He was arrested a few weeks ago and he was always loudly talking about the outrageous escapades he found himself in. But mostly he just seemed like a normal dude. Pretty young, maybe my age? Tragically he had a young son who will now grow up without a father. I could see they really loved each other, and I'm sure Louis was happiest when his boy was around. I remember him urging his son to grow up to become a hockey player.

Life is so short. People come and go. They live and they die. And then… they're gone, and who knows? Something? Nothing? Late last night I dreamed Louis was standing in our living room, draped in white cloth like Casey Affleck in *A Ghost Story*, watching Julia and I sleep, stumbling around the apartment complex, searching for closure.

Recently Watched: *The River Wild*

SUNDAY, JULY 23RD 2017 **(Woods)**
Went to Comic-Con with Julia. Stood ten feet away from Steven Spielberg as he signed autographs for *Ready Player One*. Saw costumes on display at Wētā for our friend Ian Fried's movie *Spectral*. Bought dice for D&D. Swung up to Buena Park to hit Portillo's, then caught our friend Jay Lee in Shakespeare's *The Tempest*. Stayed up until 3am to watch replay of USA gold cup game (they won!). Followed that extremely long day with soccer on Sunday (first Morning United game – we won!). And lastly, *Tintin* at the Beck's on their new badass projector.

Recently Watched: *The Adventures of Tintin, Last Chance U, Dunkirk*

TUESDAY, JULY 25TH 2017 **(Woods)**
Marathon day of writing on *Station*. Worked from 8:30am until 7pm. It's almost like this is a real job, ha. All things considered I'm very happy with this initial pass, but Scott will let me know if we're on track or not.

THURSDAY, JULY 27TH 2017 **(Woods)**
Scott liked the first flashback! Haven't really been inspired to write since delivering. Painfully slow day at the office today. Facebook.

Twitter. Deadline. Instagram. Repeat. Just counting the hours until I can leave at 7. Haven't done anything to the script outside of deleting strikethroughs. We have a major page count issue because of the stylish formatting, and will have to kill some darlings soon. Too intimidated to start writing the mid-point scenes because I know that's where many of the revisions will live, not to mention there is a lot of confusion and nebulous expectation from the filmmakers on that material, and if we don't deliver there, it will all be for nothing.

Fuck, the producers literally just checked in on our progress. Said the financier was asking. Currently cancelling any and all plans. Didn't have any. That was easy.

Re-read *A Quiet Place* during a fit of procrastination. It was depressing. The script by itself, as a piece of writing, feels disappointing and insignificant.

The Iowa Film Office invited me and Scott to do a Q&A in Iowa in August. I remember attending those awards ceremonies and events as a teenager. Looking up to Midwest filmmakers like Max Allan Collins and Stu Pollard. Hungry for any piece of advice they could share. Excited to go home and see my family and friends briefly before heading off to make *Haunt*.

Recently Watched: *Money Monster, Wind Chill*

FRIDAY, AUGUST 4TH 2017 **(Beck)**
Still waiting for our start date on *Haunt*. They're kicking around different budgets and locations, but we're in a standstill. Super frustrating, and wondering if the reality of this movie will vanish.

Recently Watched: *American Graffiti, Last Action Hero, Fast Times at Ridgemont High*

SATURDAY, AUGUST 5TH 2017 **(Woods)**
Haunt is in a dangerous limbo. Our producers have been unable to present a budget to the financier that they're willing to greenlight.

We're starting to get skeptical we'll be able to launch this project by October.

Recently Watched: *Solaris, The Graduate (x2), Last Chance U (Season 2), Salinger, Jungle Book, Game of Thrones, My Scientology Movie*

THURSDAY, AUGUST 10TH 2017 **(Woods)**

Just got done meeting Dan Trachtenberg. Incredibly nice guy. He has an overall deal at Sony TV and our agents thought because we also have Sony deal there could be some synergy. They were right, so much overlapping taste and cinema love. We are all going to put our heads together and see if we can find a way to collaborate.

I journal from time to time about procrastinating and putting work off. But never about when we're working our asses off. So.... let the record show... we've been working our asses off this week. Pulling 16 hour days. Burning the midnight oil. Don't have a lot to show for it other than blood, sweat, and tears. Becoming increasingly terrified that we can't deliver on time. But damn it all we are trying!!

Recently Watched: *10 Cloverfield Lane, Portal (short)*

TUESDAY, AUGUST 15TH 2017 **(Woods)**

I've been awake for almost 24 hours.

Scott & I have been pulling a string of all-nighters to finish a rough pass of a previously commissioned rewrite in time to meet with the director of the project while he's in LA.

I have never been more unsure about delivering a script in my career. Let's start with the fact that we're slow writers and didn't have enough time to do a pass we were happy with. Less than five weeks, while gearing up for *Haunt*, and a few other things in the wings. We both just read it all-in for the first time tonight, two hours before delivering, and neither of us were impressed. I would be freaking out right now if I wasn't so tired. The thematic ideas are all over the map.

I'm not joking when I ask, can we please just return the money and walk away?

Recently Watched: (I've watched NOTHING because all I do is write), *Ex Machina*

FRIDAY, AUGUST 18TH 2017 **(Woods)**

After flirting with Canada for several months, looks like we are heading to Kentucky for *Haunt*. Doesn't matter to us, as long as they sell KFC. Nancy Nayor our casting director is off and running. Pieces are finally starting to come together and I feel like actual prep is now only a week or two away.

Recently Watched: *Prometheus, Dark Star, Let There Be Light: The Odyssey of Dark Star*

MONDAY, AUGUST 21ST 2017 **(Woods)**

Had a call with line producer in Kentucky today. Sounds pretty on the ball. Mark warned us our financier continues to have problems with the length of the first act (i.e. the character development). I guess we've been "scaring" everyone with our references to *Dazed and Confused* and they need us to "play the game" – i.e. keep talking about how this will be the scariest movie of all time and stop talking about character.

Recently Watched: *The Strangers, Prometheus, Alien: Covenant, Wildling, Logan Lucky, Kong: Skull Island, Wind River*

FRIDAY, SEPTEMBER 8TH 2017 **(Woods)**

It's all happening. Traveling to Kentucky this week with producer Mark Fasano and our recently hired production designer Austin Gorg, who art directed what are (for our money) the best Production Design/Art Direction work in the past five years: *Her, The Neon Demon, La La Land,* and *Midnight Special*. This guy has worked on so many incredible films, with such a high level of taste and execution, that we're betting on him to take our movie to the next level. DP search isn't going as well.

A Quiet Place started preliminary photography (not principal photography).

Recently Watched: *Casting JonBenet, Get Me Roger Stone*

WEDNESDAY, SEPTEMBER 13TH 2017 **(Woods)**

Fuck. Our best hope for a haunt location just fell through. We're on the ground in Kentucky hiring crew. All week everyone has been overly optimistic the Ludlow Warehouse (which we all agreed is straight out of the script and our only great option for the haunt) was a sure thing. Sure enough we got a hard "NO" from the owners one hour ago. If we don't find a realistic backup location fast, *Haunt* is in danger of having the plug pulled.

Oh, I turn 33 tomorrow...

Recently Watched: *It, Project Greenlight (Season 4), Marauders, Dazed and Confused, Making "Dazed", Project Greenlight (Season 2), Split, We Are What We Are, The Defiant Ones*

SATURDAY, SEPTEMBER 23RD 2017 **(Woods)**

What a difference a week makes. Not only did the off-limits location come through, but we found an even better place to film – an old milk factory that has elevation changes, lots of character for the "behind the scenes" sequences, and an overwhelming amount of stage space to build sets.

Our fantastic DP Ryan Samul arrives early next week. Scott and I are sprinting through the script today to board and block so that we can be prepared to speak with him. Feel way behind on visualizing the film.

Casting is going well. Found several strong candidates for Harper. A couple Bailey's that we love. And one great Evan. No clue who the financiers would "approve" out of that list, as they've been a bit unpredictable.

Local casting is tougher. Hoping to find a few diamonds in the rough.

Went to Dent Haunted Schoolhouse – a popular local haunted house attraction in Cincinnati – last night with our 1st AD and Art team. It was fun! Some impressive sets and gags, but leans heavily on sensory assault traps which is the opposite of what we're doing in the film. Ate Pizza Hut afterwards and now I'm sick to my stomach.

A Quiet Place is 1/3 of the way through filming. We've heard they may be behind schedule, which is delaying our set visit window to the end of the shoot – which will likely make it impossible for us since we'll be directing *Haunt*.

Recently Watched: *Evil Dead, Don't Breathe, Mother!, La La Land, Contagion, The Sixth Sense, Sleight, Unbreakable, Project Greenlight*

FRIDAY, SEPTEMBER 28TH 2017 **(Beck)**

I'm now inside my new home; a Residence Inn in Erlanger, Kentucky. Yep, I'm here on location to prep *Haunt*. We start three weeks from Monday and I'm already riding the huge fucking roller coaster of ups and downs. Problem is, most of filmmaking consists of the "downs".

For instance, today we found out that the film is being bonded – a term I've always heard, but never truly realized how invasive that process is. Basically, the bond company thinks our script is too ambitious, considering our 24-day shooting schedule and our budget. We originally had 25 days to shoot this film, but somehow our contingency allotment got trimmed out, which means the red flags went up and the bond company is breathing over our necks. So now, all of the problems fall on Bryan and me.

We had a big A&E worthy "intervention" this morning, where all our production heads came together to discuss how we can trim 13 pages out of the script. That'd be a pretty ridiculous request if we were months out from production, but now we're three weeks out – so that request became <u>fucking</u> ridiculous.

Now we have new problems hanging over our heads of how to make a good movie while cutting character, stunts, spectacle, etc.

I'm starting to remember how shitty movies are still made with good intentions. We haven't cast a single person yet and we're waaaaay behind on storyboarding.

Recently Watched: *Cast Away, Everybody Wants Some!!*

SATURDAY, SEPTEMBER 30TH 2017 **(Woods)**

Deep in prep. No time to journal. They just yanked two more days from our schedule. We created a dart board with the Bond Company Stooge from *The Life Aquatic* in our production office.

Met Moises Arias (Biaggio from *Kings of Summer*) for the part of Evan. Great dude. He seemed really freaked out by the script in a good way.

Also circling Erin Moriarty (also from *Kings of Summer*) for the part of Harper. She has a conflict right now with another film. We have five BRILLIANT options for Harper waiting in the wings and we're still watching tape and auditioning!

Watched *Neighbors 2* on TV and this young comedic actress caught our eye for a potential Angela. She goes by Awkwafina, and our casting director will be tracking her down this week.[11]

Recently Watched: *You're Next, La La Land, Magnolia, The Royal Tenenbaums, Neighbors 2, It Comes at Night, It*

SUNDAY, OCTOBER 8TH 2017 **(Woods)**

A dog barking in the next room woke me up early. I watched *La La Land* for the 100th time (it just plays on repeat on HBO).

We officially have our Harper: Katie Stevens!

She really blew us away in her taped audition, and even more so after the fact when we interviewed her on Skype. She lobbied and fought for the role, and in the end, that kind of hard work and enthusiasm

---

[11] Two years later, Awkwafina would star in *The Farewell*, one of our favorite movies of 2019.

goes a really long way, which ultimately helped her edge out our long-time front runner.

We start filming in two weeks. Scott and I are marathoning through the storyboarding process, still so far behind. Our office wall is starting to shape up…

Recently Watched: *La La Land, Spielberg (documentary), Magnolia*

TUESDAY, OCTOBER 10TH 2017 (Woods)

Writing this from the back of a scout van. A week and a half away from shooting. We just learned there will be no video playback on set. Apparently, because of the union, you have to *hire* someone to control playback. This individual is extremely expensive. Scott and I are confused. We've been making movies since we were kids. We've never made a movie without "playing back a take" because the technology makes it so easy anyone can do it.

We are under pressure to cast more actors locally. Everyone's budgets are coming in too high. I don't know how we're supposed to pull this movie off. Trying to stay positive and keep my eye on the "donut, not the hole" – David Lynch's advice to Eli Roth back in the day.

No clue if we're shooting anamorphic or wimping out and going spherical again. We love the anamorphic look, but there are so many limitations in our tight haunt hallways.

MONDAY, OCTOBER 23RD 2017 **(Beck)**

We direct *Haunt* in four hours. I don't know what I ate yesterday that made my stomach so upset. I'm sitting here in a dark hotel room, with 100% chance of rain outside my window. I feel about as ready as I can be, but my stomach is in knots. I was totally fine last night, but the inevitable anxiety got to me. Hoping our exterior shots won't be a bust due to the rain, but I'm already embracing the fact that we may not get all our pieces. I feel like we're heading into a gauntlet – much more than past productions – considering all of the insane variables of this production. It came together so quickly, I'm not convinced we're as prepared as we should be.

MONDAY, OCTOBER 23RD 2017 **(Woods)**

First day of filming is tomorrow. I'm so nervous. Nervous about the whole schedule. If I'm being honest, it seems like there's only five or six days that are makeable on this schedule, tomorrow being one of them.[12] The rest feel close to impossible days. If we don't make tomorrow, we're completely fucked.[13] My hope for our first day... that we have fun. That we make something special. That our crew works hard for us, and that in turn we treat them with the respect and kindness they deserve. I am so lucky. This is my life. My family and friends have worked so hard for me to be able to do what I love for a living and I cannot take it for granted.

Recently Watched: *Green Room, Nocturnal Animals, Happy Gilmore*

TUESDAY, OCTOBER 24TH 2017 **(Woods)**

My entire back went out the morning of Day 1. It was like a ghost beat me with a baseball bat in my hotel room. I literally screamed and keeled over. No one was around. Must be all that stress and pressure. The crew took care of me and by the end of the day I was able to walk.

Weirdest thing ever.

---

[12] It wasn't.
[13] We were.

FRIDAY, OCTOBER 27ᵀᴴ 2017 **(Woods)**

Day five of filming. Four in the can. I don't sleep more than five hours a night, but I seem to have more energy now than I do when I'm in writer mode, napping and watching soccer all day.

The actors are incredible. There were a few tough scenes on day one that I wish we could get back. We hadn't gotten used to working together yet, and were kind of shooting in the dark, trying to wring performances out of them and burning up a lot of time for very little coverage. Our assistant director blew a gasket pretty early on: "I don't want to be a dick, but we can't move at this pace." Lauryn feels the scene out for the first few takes and once she warms up she's a rockstar. Shazi always gives you something you don't expect. Will needs the freedom to use his instincts. Katie is a total pro, likes to be part of the conversation and talk through motivation. Andrew acts as if he's been waiting for this role his entire life. And Schuyler is a revelation. Easy to direct, always ready to dive in and look silly. We love working with this cast.

Every day has been a mountain to climb. Averaging between 36-40 setups a day, with six main characters that have to be covered. Our DP Ryan Samul and his team are doing tremendous work.

Recently Watched: *Carnival of Souls, Gone Girl, Halloween 5, Lady in the Water, Donnie Darko, Making of Donnie Darko, Making of Funny People, Making of The Lovely Bones*

SATURDAY, OCTOBER 28ᵀᴴ 2017 **(Beck)**

We wrapped week one of production on *Haunt* only one hour and twenty-three minutes ago. I have to admit... it feels damn good. A helluva lot better than I thought it would be. That's not to say this week was easy – it was anything BUT. The first three days were fucking insane, as we were shooting way too many pages a day with way too many characters. It was a fucking marathon to get through those long hours, but we made it. These actors are fantastic, and the scary sequences we shot yesterday and today (spider room and laboratory) were so fun to direct. On the ride home from set today,

Bryan & I spoke about how today felt like the first time in YEARS that we truly felt the filmmaking bug again. Can't believe we've already shot 30 pages of the script, and I can't wait to get into week two. I feel very lucky and fortunate to be in this position to make this movie.

SATURDAY, NOVEMBER 4TH 2017 **(Woods)**

Two weeks in the can. Last couple days have been hard. Went double overtime on the tunnel day. We were so nimble on our camera tests while shooting the tunnels that we thought it would be easy, but that was just a T-Section, and we quickly learned that selling a larger piece of tunnels as different sections required a lot of different lighting setups and maneuvering around – plus we owed the back half of the slide scene from previous day. Once we got to the dungeon, things picked back up until the smoke gag malfunctioned, costing us an extra hour of resets and probably an obscene amount of money. We lost our cool a little bit, and our cast reached out the following day to apologize… they thought we were mad at them. They've done such a great job, really going above and beyond, and there's no doubt that they are trying to make the best movie possible. We made sure to let them know our frustrations were about other things.

Our agent Dan and manager Ryan visited set this week. They told us someone made an offer on an old script we wrote years ago but they are advising us to pass – they think it could be more valuable in the long run if we hang onto it and do it right. Ryan mentioned one of his industry colleagues has read Shyamalan's script for *Glass* (which is shooting right now)… apparently he did NOT like the script. That gives me peace actually. Means I'll probably love it.

Watching *The Royal Tenenbaums* right now and it is so goddamn inspiring and I'm realizing that even though we make horror films, I think the director that influences our work the most might be… Wes Anderson?

Recently Watched: *The Fog, The Royal Tenenbaums, Halloween III: Season of the Witch*

FRIDAY, NOVEMBER 10TH 2017 (Woods)

Just watched our editor Terel's first assembly of the opening five minutes of the film. It was a completely sobering moment. We are terrible directors. Our last-minute choices for the bedroom set look godawful. Green walls? Ugly fake wall in the hallway that looks like a damn office at Terracon.[14] The lighting for anything looking towards the door is too CW. Everything looking inside the room is solid. Unfortunately we spend most the scene looking the bad way. Our stilted camera choices and blocking throttled the performances and honestly we just weren't ready for this important of a scene on day one of photography. Terel is doing a *great* job but we're not giving him the goods.

Had a call with the financiers minutes after watching the assembly. Had to pretend we were unbelievably happy about everything we've gotten so far. Wonder if they could tell that we are actually terrified we've fucked up the whole film.

Recently Watched: *Speed, Evil Dead*

SUNDAY, NOVEMBER 12TH 2017 (Woods)

It's been so fun watching our old friend Justin Marxen become the Clown. All of the monsters have brought something really special to their roles. Chaney Morrow was a manager at Waffle House two weeks ago and now he's giving a masterclass in acting on set every day as the Ghost. Damien Maffei is completely menacing as the Devil. Schuyler White as Zombie and Jessi Fisher as the Witch have really impressed with their physicality. And holy hell the makeup FX team have given us all nightmares. Chris Bridges and Hugo Villaseñor are doing next-level work. The conceit was to create monsters that were even scarier once the masks came off, hopefully turning the slasher trope of a masked villain on its head. But that could so easily have gotten cheesy. Most of our conversations have been outside of the horror genre. We've talked a lot about the realism of Michael Mann

---

[14] Terracon is an office where Scott's dad used to work. We shot all of our homemade movies there when we were kids.

and asked Chris & Hugo to think of these guys as if they were criminals in *Thief* or *Heat*, rather than Tobe Hooper's *The Funhouse*. They've done such a great job creating something beautiful, specific, and grounded with each character.

Recently Watched: *Superbad, Hearts of Darkness: A Filmmaker's Apocalypse, American Movie, It Follows*

THURSDAY, NOVEMBER 23ʳᴰ 2017 (Woods)

Thanksgiving. Lot to be thankful for this year. Wrapped *Haunt* last night. Burned down the oil corridor in a blaze of glory with our friend and collaborator of fifteen years, Justin Marxen, who played the Clown. Probably the greatest joy of the entire production was working with him and seeing how excited he was to be on a real film set working side by side with class actors. His dad would be so fucking proud.

I am running on fumes. Haven't slept in 2 ½ months. It was all worth it. So much more satisfying shooting a film that's *not* from the point of view of a flashlight like *Nightlight*.[15] I have no clue if we did a good job, but the cast & crew gave us their all every single day.

A Quiet Place trailer dropped and has already tallied 4.5 million views. We can't believe how perfectly it captures the script. Got to see the trailer in front of *Justice League* at our hometown movie theater, Cinema 53ʳᵈ, where I saw *The Sixth Sense* and first knew I wanted to write movies. This is the stuff dreams are made of.

Resting and relaxing for the next few days in Iowa. Happy Joe's and movies with my family. *Legends of the Hidden Temple* and Rudy's with my friends. Then on Monday... back to work.

Recently Watched: *Justice League, Stranger Things, Ocean's Eleven*

---

[15] *Nightlight* was conceived in the heyday of found footage and POV-driven films. The central gimmick devised to help set the film apart was having the entire story unfold from the POV of a young woman's haunted flashlight. Judging by the 14% on RottenTomatoes.com, we may not have pulled it off.

MONDAY, DECEMBER 4TH 2017 (Beck)

I'm inside St. John's Hospital in Santa Monica, watching my wife hold my newborn child. People say becoming a parent changes your life, and while I understand that, I would better describe it as "evolves" your life. I don't feel different, but I do feel my understanding of my priorities, the concept of the world, and the meaning of life to all be expanded. This feeling is hard to quantify, but I will say I'm beyond grateful to have a healthy kid and healthy wife relaxing in front of me. I will eternally remember what it felt like when my daughter first looked at me in the operating room.

It's been a marathon to have jumped straight into fatherhood after directing *Haunt*. In fact, I can't believe the last entry I made was after only the first week of production. That film was insane from every perspective and many many times I thought we were going to be royally fucked by unforeseen screw-ups or tight scheduling. The crew was phenomenal and held in there, and I'm somewhat in disbelief that we came in on schedule. So many nights were freezing cold with way too many pages and way too many setups. But we did it. I'll need to recap on production a little more later, when I don't have an infant by my side.

Recently Watched: *Dick Tracy*

TUESDAY, DECEMBER 5TH 2017 (Woods)

Scott added Baby Beck to the family this weekend!!! A beautiful baby girl!!!

Saw *Phantom Thread* at the DGA theater in Los Angeles. Rian Johnson moderated a Q&A. PTA is still a giant. His films are brave and hold a unique power over me. Totally loved all the Hitchcock allusions. And the Daniel Day-Lewis character felt embarrassingly personal. PTA always puts his gut on the page. So inspiring.

The *Haunt* rough edits continue to roll in like a punch to the face. Terel is doing a wonderful job, he's a great editor, afraid we just didn't give him the goods to work with. I think we'll find out quickly in

January how fucked we really are, but as always… I'm preparing for the worst.

Supposedly Screen Gems and Dark Castle are now interested in an old spec script of ours that never sold. We've heard this many times over the years. People keep getting re-excited about that project any time we catch a wave of buzz. And then eventually it goes away.

Recently Watched: *Zodiac, American Vandal, Mindhunter (Season 1), Phantom Thread*

WEDNESDAY, DECEMBER 6ᵀᴴ 2017 (Woods)

Got some fun news… *A Quiet Place* was named one of the 10 BEST SPEC SCRIPTS by the 2017 Hit List.

Justin Marxen called and said: "Bryan, do you remember about 8 years ago… we were in Iowa sitting in front of your computer. And you were showing me this list of all the best spec scripts in the business. And you told me… 'one day I hope we're on that list.' Dude. You're on that fucking list!" I thought it was nice of him to remind me what an egomaniac I am.

Recently Watched: *Alien 3*

TUESDAY, DECEMBER 19ᵀᴴ 2017 (Woods)

I'm writing this from West Linn, Oregon, at Julia's family's house for Christmas. The *A Quiet Place* trailer is playing in front of the new Star Wars movie. A dream come true.

Recently Watched: *Star Wars: The Last Jedi, Star Wars: The Force Awakens, Downsizing, Vice Principles (Season 1), A Christmas Story: Live, The Witch*

TUESDAY, JANUARY 2ᴺᴰ 2018 (Beck)

Happy New Year. The rough assembly of *Haunt* is paused on my screen. I haven't touched it yet and, in fact, have been dreading this moment for a long, long time… but the band-aid has to be ripped off. I just treated myself to a feast of pizza, and will be drinking a

Kentucky mule with a side of sour gummy bears to help mend my sorrows while undergoing the torture of this rough assembly. Godspeed.

Recently Watched: *Alice ('90), Last Flag Flying, Darkest Hour, Good Time, A Ghost Story, The Beguiled, All These Sleepless Nights*

TUESDAY, JANUARY 2ND 2018 **(Woods)**
Currently watching the rough assembly of *Haunt* and want to die.

Recently Watched: *Haunt, Star Wars: Rogue One, Star Wars: A New Hope, The Emperor's New Groove, Holes*

THURSDAY, JANUARY 4TH 2018 **(Woods)**
Scott and I went through the rough assembly of *Haunt* together today. There's about six sequences that are terrible. We agree that the ███████████ sequence is the worst in the movie, and are worried it won't get much better. That hurts the entire movie, because if that doesn't work than everything else is pointless. We also have no idea if the movie will be scary. Currently it's not. There are a few entertaining sequences, and it feels somewhat cool at times, but not *remotely* scary. Ask me again in two months.

Recently Watched: *The Shape of Water, Three Billboards Outside Ebbing Missouri, Star Wars: Attack of the Clones, Star Wars, Revenge of the Sith, All the Money in the World, The Disaster Artist, Haunt, Happy Death Day, Picture This*

MONDAY, JANUARY 8TH 2018 **(Woods)**
First day of our director's cut with our editor Terel Gibson (*The Kings of Summer*). We fought hard to hire Terel and it was all worth it. What a cool, talented person to spend a day locked in a room with. Incredible hire. Time to piece this thing together little by little.

Watched the Golden Globes alone yesterday. Happy for *Three Billboards* (which is brilliant), but *Get Out* is clearly the film of the year.

FRIDAY, JANUARY 12ᵀᴴ 2018 **(Woods)**

Editing has been so much fun. It's a lot of work and there are many scenes we have completely fucked up, but who cares. This is what we love to do.

Saw Shazi Raja in *Brad's Status* and was blown away. She played a completely different character than Angela in *Haunt* and really came alive. Fun to see. The film was a really interesting double feature with the terrific *Lady Bird*. Both movies centering around parents and their kids.

Playing "Betrayal At Hill House" the board game tonight with my D&D friends. Hoping to wrangle some inspiration for a potential movie adaptation that Hasbro likes us for.

Recently Watched: *Brad's Status, M, Lady Bird, Call Me By Your Name*

FRIDAY, JANUARY 19ᵀᴴ 2018 **(Woods)**

Brought our producers into the editing room to share a scene from *Haunt* yesterday. Showed them the "Guess the Body Parts" sequence. They didn't seem too impressed. One of them checked their phone *twice* during the scene. The other didn't say a word. We're very nervous. Can't tell if we're being overly sensitive.

In surreal news, we just got approached to rewrite Damien Chazelle's next movie.

As I write this, we are working on the coffin sequence with Terel. It's been much harder to crack than we imagined. The scene as a whole isn't terrible, but many parts of it don't land.

The rough assembly is better than what we've been able to put together. And we *hated* the assembly.

Recently Watched: *John Adams, Before I Wake, Black Mirror: USS Callister*

MONDAY, JANUARY 22ND 2018 **(Woods)**

Reading Eleanor Coppola's "Notes" again. It's her diary of the making of *Apocalypse Now*. Wow, she's my hero. Provides such devastating insight into what it's like to be married to a self-indulgent artist.

Someone should make a movie about *her*.

SUNDAY, FEBRUARY 4TH, 2018 **(Woods)**

Super Bowl Sunday. About to check off an insane bucket list item that I never dreamed of putting on my bucket list to begin with because it's so completely absurd....

Paramount spent $5 million to air
a Super Bowl trailer for A Quiet Place!!!

Just learned the film will be opening the SXSW film festival. Still trying to process the news. Julia's documentary *Fail State* is playing at SXSW EDU, which means we both have films playing. So cool.

Recently Watched: *Mosaic, In a Valley of Violence, Blade Runner 2049*

A Quiet Place billboard on Sunset Boulevard in Los Angeles
near the ***Haunt*** editing offices.

THURSDAY, FEBRUARY 8TH 2018 (Woods)

Doing the press kit interviews tomorrow on the Paramount lot for *A Quiet Place*.

Had our friend Kurt Oberhaus over to show him a few scenes from *Haunt* (he played a PA at the party). Couldn't really gauge his reaction. His non-reaction has sent me into a nervous spiral. Could tell he dug some of the Evan improv. But that's about it. Are these scenes bad?

Recently Watched: *Mosaic, Gone Girl, Night of the Living Dead, Night of Anubis (workprint cut of Night of the Living Dead), Wish Upon, 47 Meters Down, Black Panther, Young Mr. Lincoln, Super Dark Times*

TUESDAY, FEBRUARY 27TH 2018 (Woods)

Last night was miserable. Screened a rough cut of *Haunt* for our significant others. I could tell they were straining to find nice things to say about it. Julia yawned three times during the movie. Christy felt the first act was too "CW". They had the same panicked look on their faces that Scott and I probably had watching the first assembly. The movie doesn't work. Of course it doesn't work. It's a rough cut, that's a given, I remind myself.

Recently Watched: *Haunt*

SUNDAY, MARCH 4TH 2018 (Woods)

Watching the Oscars tonight at the Becks. Rooting for *Get Out*.

Recently Watched: *Death Wish ('18), Lights Out, Haunt*

THURSDAY, MARCH 15TH 2018 (Woods)

Holy shit so much has happened. We're in Texas and my brother and sister-in-law and I got to see Julia's documentary *Fail State* play at the Alamo Ritz. I ordered some delicious chicken tenders and watched Dan Rather himself introduce the film. It played remarkably well on the big screen with a sold-out audience. I was so proud of Julia and moved once again by the film itself. The rest of the week was spent playing disc golf at an amazing course that had all kinds of gimmick holes like mini golf, competing in "Bang" and a hilarious dice game called "Can't Stop", all building up to the premiere of *A Quiet Place*.

On premiere night, Scott & I did an interview with Deadline Hollywood and then walked the red carpet. Afterwards we got ushered to the green room where we saw John and Emily, who were being mobbed by lots of people so we didn't say hello. They did such an unbelievable job with the movie. We did however meet Millicent Simmonds for the first time, who is such a lovely person. Then we caught up with our producers who were sweating bullets, but trying to play it cool. I guess we were all terrified about the screening.

Finally we took our seats and the lights went down. With the VFX, sound mix and score in, the film had totally come to life in a way we hadn't experienced before. You could feel the audience was ready to go for a ride. They laughed, they screamed, and some may have even cried. Did the very end of the movie work? Hard to read! But reaction seemed fairly positive.

During the Q&A, a woman from our hometown of Bettendorf, Iowa got on the mic, demanded to know where the screenwriters were, and proceeded to tell the audience about her writing career or something. Eventually someone wrestled the mic away from her. That was awkward for all of us.

The highlight of the whole trip was spending a solid 45 minutes talking to Michael Bay at the after party. He wasn't what I expected. He was soft-spoken, passionate about his work and the work on the film, and incredibly generous with his time. We assaulted him with questions about *Pain & Gain*, and he regaled us with stories of all the biggest stars he's worked with, before finally turning the microscope onto us.

He asked us how we felt about the cut, and he mentioned a scene that got a "bad laugh" both at the screening we just left, as well as the test screening the night before. He asked us how to fix it, and we pitched a line that could be trimmed to help.[16]

It's been a few days now since we've been back. *A Quiet Place* currently has a 100% on Rotten Tomatoes with 24 reviews counted. The studio couldn't be happier and everyone is now expecting the film to be a hit. But one of the coolest things this week....

Eli Roth watched and loved *Haunt*.

Recently Watched: *Fail State, A Quiet Place, The Strangers: Prey at Night, Split, Summer '03, Isle of Dogs, Dog Bites Man, Haunt*

FRIDAY, MARCH 16TH 2018 (Beck)

We got a beautiful call from Eli Roth. In his words "THE CUT IS FUCKING TERRIFYING." It was very nice to get these words of encouragement when we're so deep in the edit, on top of the strange world we're living in with *A Quiet Place*.

Recently Watched: *The Strangers: Prey at Night, Summer '03*

TUESDAY, MARCH 20TH 2018 (Woods)

First Friends & Family screening of *Haunt* happened last night. Still feeling a little sick. Don't know what to make of it. The feedback cards still haven't come in. The humor fell pretty flat in the second act. Several scares definitely worked. But I don't know. The smattering of forced applause at the end was muted. Everyone we talked to afterwards was complimentary, but cold.

Immediately after the screening an email came in with *Boogeyman* notes. Our producers want to be pitching in two weeks. FML.

p.s. Scott, Kurt, and I finally went to Wahlburgers, the Mark/Donnie burger restaurant that has its own reality show. We had been joking about going there for months, ever since it opened on Sunset Blvd.

---

[16] The team eventually massaged this moment after SXSW, thus fixing the problem. It was a reminder that sometimes the smallest edits can have a large impact.

Well… we went and the joke was on us: they happened to be filming an episode of the show. So we signed our lives away and ate burgers while Donnie Wahlberg trotted around mugging for the camera. Hilarious.

Recently Watched: *Haunt, Nerve, Annihilation, Dog Bites Man*

THURSDAY, MARCH 22ND 2018 **(Beck)**
Currently sitting here in the American Airlines VIP lounge to catch a flight for the *A Quiet Place* press conference in Manhattan and I can't believe the sole reason I'm here (and about to sit in a $5,400 seat in First Class) is because Bryan & I wrote a script to shoot for $100,000 in Iowa. I mean, this is fucking excessive. There's a huge buffet of free food, along with champagne (which people are partaking in even though it's 7 in the fucking AM). I'll enjoy it while it lasts, but this would be an unsustainable existence to only travel this way. It's way out of touch. And it's way too quiet up in this lounge considering this is an airport.

We did our first *Haunt* friends and family screening on Monday. Some things fell completely flat while others got the intended reaction. Got a ton of feedback, so now we're off to battle, once again, which is the primary focus of this job… battle the script development, battle the pre-production process, battle the lack of shooting days, battle the edit. At least we have a great editor who is a fucking joy to work with. That makes this process much more bearable.

Recently Watched: *Mud*

FRIDAY, MARCH 30TH 2018 **(Woods)**
This is the busiest I've ever been in my life. We are editing *Haunt* every day, and battling to get a day of pickups. We are traveling with *A Quiet Place* for the impending release. Leave New York tomorrow for the premiere and press. Then next week we head back to Iowa for more screenings and press. All the while I've had to carve out time to work on my proposal to Julia. Wrote three chapters of *Harry Potter* fan-fiction that ends with popping the question. I'm not

good with traditional prose, way different than screenwriting, so it was a challenge. Also, I'm not that into *Harry Potter.*

Recently Watched: *It Happened One Night, Never Let Me Go*

MONDAY, APRIL 2ND 2018 (Beck)

I'm sitting in my Manhattan hotel room as my daughter sits at my feet. She is constantly smiling at me. I'm an incredibly lucky person to have her in my life. We're here for the official premiere of *A Quiet Place*, which starts in three hours. There was a beautiful April snow that fell this morning as Christy & I enjoyed breakfast in bed, listening to Christmas songs and hanging with our daughter as she laughed and smiled. My daughter also just had a massive shart which took 12 minutes to completely clean up, but that didn't phase me. I'm just really happy, all things considered. I never thought Bryan & I would experience this, as much as I had hoped we would throughout the years. This has been a terrific trip, and I'm quite at peace. Enjoy the moment – that's what I'm thinking every second.

TUESDAY, APRIL 3RD 2018 (Woods)

Just got home from NYC. What an incredible weekend. First of all, Julia and I got engaged. Julia Glausi, my future wife, read three chapters of my *Harry Potter* fan-fiction, laughing and crying the whole way through, and then accepted my ring. We stayed at the Whitby. I must have taken five baths because the bathtub had a television in the wall. Paramount covered all of our expenses, so we loaded up on mini-bar snacks and room service. Saw the Broadway play "Three Tall Women" which absolutely blew me away. Then all the festivities began. Rolled up to the red carpet wearing suits and gowns. Did several interviews for Hollywood Reporter, Entertainment Tonight, E! Television, etc. Said hello to all of our amazing guests (Scott's parents and sister Christina, Julia's fam, Ryan our *Haunt* DP, bff Shane and his lady Clare), then took our seats right in front of nobodies like Blake Lively, Ryan Reynolds, and Justin Theroux. Movie played well. No surprise there as it's a premiere audience. Signed some autographs after the festivities. Then meandered around the after party. Finally got to meet composer Marco Beltrami and talked shop. Avoided the fancy people as best we could. Then grabbed some delicious New York style pizza.

Bryan Woods and his fiancé Julia, moments after their engagement in New York City.

Scott, his wife Christy, and daughter on a flight to the *A Quiet Place* premiere in New York City.

Haunt screens again Thursday night. Eli told us he invited Ti *FUCKING* West – a filmmaker I greatly admire. He's no hack and will surely see right through our bullshit.[17]

Also, we revised the third act per Eli's idea – without shooting a single new frame. Very curious to see how that will color the audience's reaction.

We need something bold to move the needle. The last cut of the movie was just not delivering a satisfying finale. Here's hoping.

Recently Watched: *Haunt, A Quiet Place, The Hateful Eight, Unsane*

TUESDAY, APRIL 10TH 2018 (Woods)

A Quiet Place opening weekend. We demolished all expectations (except my Dad's, lol) by opening to #1 with a $50 million dollar weekend. The film got strong reviews, awards buzz, and played to sold out crowds at our home town. Stephen King tweeted that he loved the film. What the hell!?

Thursday night we screened a rough cut of *Haunt* for friends & family. Friday we introduced *A Quiet Place* to a sold out audience at the AMC Century City where we used to work. Hard to comprehend.

On Saturday we flew to Iowa and watched the film with the hometown crowd. My brother Jason showed up by surprise at the last minute, and I was so grateful to have (for maybe the first time ever), my ENTIRE family present in the room (Chris, Denny, Meg, Jay and on and on). Sat next to my mom as she sobbed through the pregnancy sequence which she had read on the page only a year ago.

Emails and Facebook posts and tweets continue to pour in. All of ICM has emailed us congratulations.[18] As I type this, I received a text from our Sound Designer on *Haunt*, Mac Smith, who said the

---

[17] Ti West is the writer/director of *The Innkeepers, The Sacrament,* and our personal favorite, *The House of the Devil.*
[18] Our agent Daniel Cohan moved from WME to ICM.

screening of *A Quiet Place* last night at Skywalker Ranch was a big success.

Scott Beck and Bryan Woods introducing *A Quiet Place* on opening night at AMC Century City where they used to work.

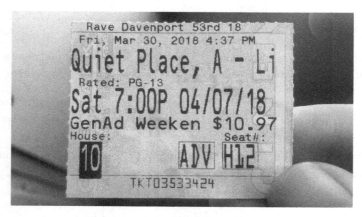

A Quiet Place ticket stub from the writers' hometown movie theater in Davenport, Iowa.

At a time when our career could not be hotter, I also feel like it is ending. We are struggling with *Haunt*, as audiences continue to reject both the beginning and ending. Ti West seemed unimpressed by the film, and compared it to *Puppet Master*.[19] He said that was a compliment, but was it? He told us to cut down all the character stuff and just get to the haunt faster. "Save that for your next film," he said. The irony was not lost on him that his movies usually have 40-50 minutes of character development and we all laughed about it.

We will take all of his notes to heart and make the movie stronger.

Recently Watched: *A Quiet Place* (x3), *Phantom Thread, The Girl with the Dragon Tattoo (Fincher)*

THURSDAY, APRIL 12TH 2018 (Woods)

We pitch *Boogeyman* to Fox tomorrow with Madhouse and 21 Laps. And we're hearing rumblings about an *A Quiet Place* sequel. Producers want to discuss that with us, but we'd rather write the next original thing.

Recently Watched: *Rebel Without a Crew, Friday the 13th (remake), Silicon Valley, The Babadook*

MONDAY, APRIL 16TH 2018 (Woods)

We sold *Boogeyman* to Fox in less than four hours. 21 Laps said that was the fastest they ever sold a movie.

Recently Watched: *A Quiet Place, Come Sunday, Ready Player One, The Director and the Jedi (Making of The Last Jedi), Overnight*

SUNDAY, APRIL 22ND 2018 (Woods)

Tomandandy sent us their first music noodling. There's some exciting stuff. Need to keep an open mind and be willing to see the film through somebody else's eyes.

Got to attend Festival of Books with Julia for our third year. This time the only highlight was Lawrence Wright, author of "Scientology and the Prison of Belief", as well as "The Looming Tower".

---

[19] A schlocky low-budget horror film from 1989 that we enjoyed quite a bit as kids to be honest.

Darren Aronofsky was a no-show to his sold-out panel.

Recently Watched: *Tales of Halloween, The Ritual, You're Next, Beyond Skyline, War for the Planet of the Apes, A Quiet Place, Trainwreck, One Strange Rock (pilot), Roseanne*

THURSDAY, MAY 3RD 2018 **(Woods)**

Saw *Ghost Stories* this weekend, a very scary film that was beautifully directed, and it made me depressed. Hell, just watching the trailer for *Hereditary* makes me depressed. These low budget indie horror films are so much better than what we are able to put up on screen.

Negotiations on *Boogeyman* are not going well.

Our new assistant editor JP noticed that we were ripping ourselves off with the nail gag in *A Quiet Place* and *Haunt* which is awesome!

Recently Watched: *Ghost Stories, When Jeff Tries to Save the World, The Village, Mercy, Haunt*

MONDAY, MAY 9TH 2018 **(Beck)**

I'm sitting in bed in the John Steinbeck bedroom at Skywalker Ranch, and I feel like I'm at Disneyland. Outside it's completely quiet… like DEAD SILENT. It's beautiful and incredibly zen. There's a lot of catching up to do.

We're gearing up for a test screening next Wednesday and are currently doing a temp mix here at Skywalker Ranch. It's fucking Heaven. I mean, the air is totally unlike anywhere else on Earth, which is total hyperbole, but come up here and see for yourself.

I hope I can enjoy the next two days and the fact we get to work at a place like this.

Recently Watched: *Sing Street, The Fall, Jurassic Park, Trafic ('71), John Mulaney: Kid Gorgeous at Radio City, Duel, Monty Python's Life of Brian, Sweet Smell of Success*

7. How would you describe *HAUNT* to your friends? (PLEASE BE SPECIFIC)

Dope

7. How would you describe *HAUNT* to your friends? (PLEASE BE SPECIFIC)

Most Fucked up movie in a Decade.

8. If you **WOULD NOT** "DEFINITELY" recommend this movie to your friends at Question #2, why not? (PLEASE BE SPECIFIC)

It won't make Sensitive

Amusing responses from a *Haunt* test screening.

SATURDAY, JUNE 16TH 2018 (Woods)

We have a call with Lissie, a superstar musician who just happens to be from our hometown. Hoping to convince her to do a cover of "Monster Mash" for the end credits of *Haunt*. It's a tall order given that her cover of Kid Cudi's "Pursuit of Happiness" makes her the greatest cover artist in the history of music as far as I'm concerned.

Met with writer/director Nicholas Meyer this week.[20] Had a lively discussion about losing your way in the edit, how tough Gene Hackman is to work with, and the poetry of Jacques Tati. He mentioned the toll a film career can take on your personal life. This is something Scott & I worry about a lot.

After marinating on it, I think *First Reformed* is my favorite movie of the year. A late stunner from Paul Schrader that I never saw coming.

Recently Watched: *Kevin Smith: Silent But Deadly, Fourth Estate, Contracted, Twilight Zone*

THURSDAY, AUGUST 9TH 2018 (Woods)

Writing this from Skywalker Ranch, the Ansel Adams room. Our final mix day is tomorrow and we're feeling the crunch. Just heard

---

[20] Nicholas Meyer is most known for directing *Time After Time* and what is considered by many to be the best *Star Trek* film of all-time, *Star Trek II: The Wrath of Khan*.

Kathleen Kennedy wants to meet which is probably the pinnacle of our career so maybe it's time to retire.

Lissie's Rob Zombie cover is so so so excellent.[21] Our mixer Tony is a big Rob Zombie fan and he really loved her rendition and that means a lot to us.

Recently Watched: *Fog City Mavericks, The Devil Wears Prada, Haunt, Snatched*

THURSDAY, AUGUST 23RD 2018 (Woods)

About to take a Lyft to the Grove where *Haunt* will screen for every North American distributor in Los Angeles. I feel a little sick. Very nervous. Not just about the screening, but having to be social with our producers and financiers and agents beforehand. Did a QC pass of whole movie this morning and Scott's mom got to watch the film. She said she loved it and got teary eyed when our names came up at the end. On some level that's the only review that matters.

Trying to remind myself to enjoy the ride while we are lucky enough to be allowed to make movies.

Recently Watched: *Haunt, Who is America?*

THURSDAY, AUGUST 23RD 2018 (Beck)

Before tonight's *Haunt* distributor screening, Eli introduced us to film critic extraordinaire Elvis Mitchell, whom I've watched/listened to for years, including a very special interview of Christopher Nolan when he screened *Pink Floyd's The Wall* years ago in anticipation of the *Inception* release.

When I emerged from the screening, Elvis approached me and began applauding (!?). He shook my hand and said how much he enjoyed the film. He even said we should come on the show. It was an incredibly kind gesture, presumably from someone who doesn't need

---

[21] The previously recorded "Monster Mash" cover was unusable due to rights issues.

to do such things (or at least that's what I'm telling myself). This will be the highlight of the night, and one of the few highlights of this career we've embarked upon. I need to remember that it's these little gestures that I need to acknowledge and take stock of, because no matter how small, they make it all worth it.

Recently Watched: *Fog City Mavericks*

MONDAY, SEPTEMBER 24TH 2018 (Woods)

Just watched Eli Roth's *The House with a Clock in Its Walls* at the exact same theater in the Grove where *Haunt* played only a month ago. I'm happy to report that it was fucking terrific. A kid's film that's actually scary. Performances were amazing all the way around. Production design and music were gorgeous. The direction was so confident it felt like the work of an old Hollywood craftsman who had been working in the studio system for decades. Congrats Eli!

We are officially commenced on *Boogeyman*!!! Feels great. We had to give Fox a 30-minute recap pitch over the phone of the whole movie and now we're off to the races.

Recently Watched: *The House with a Clock in Its Walls, A Simple Favor, Maniac, Shutter Island, Blair Witch (remake w/commentary), Bram Stoker's Dracula, Drag Me to Hell*

THURSDAY, NOVEMBER 1ST 2018 (Beck)

The entire ride for *A Quiet Place* continues to take us into fascinating territories that I never expected. In September, we were flown to DePaul for a one-on-one discussion with Scott Myers, and I was hugely inspired by the students there. I started reminiscing about how I felt as a college student, wondering how I could navigate a career in film. Those emotions are intertwined with a frustration of not seeing a path ahead, but a naïve optimism that the entire road has yet to be paved. I returned to LA supercharged, and every morning I want to capture that momentum. And last week, we were guest panelists at the Austin Film Festival, which truly celebrates writers. The main highlight was seeing a print of *Speed* at the Alamo Drafthouse, which

I had never seen on the big screen. I fucking adore that film, and it was a pleasure to hear Graham Yost, the screenwriter, speak about his experiences. We personally told Graham how influential his work had been for us and how *A Quiet Place* wouldn't exist without *Speed*. A deeply monumental encounter, to say the least. We walked out of the Drafthouse with pure joy.

I don't know what's happening with *Haunt*, other than we've had offers from A24 and Lionsgate, among others. The biggest problem is the film won't be released for another 364 days. Who knows if it'll still be relevant by then. I'm gonna hate promoting a film that feels so far removed from our artistic headspace.

The biggest life change is that Christy and I bought a house in Iowa. We literally closed on it yesterday. We're doing this move for family, and I will dearly miss the arts, culture, diversity, and weather in Los Angeles. Both of us are convinced we'll return to the West Coast in the near future, but in the meantime, we will try to enjoy our time with loved ones. I'll have to bounce back and forth between Iowa and LA, although I have no visual projection of how that looks. Will I just be out for days at a time, once a month? Or will I have to live here for weeks at a time?

Recently Watched: *Speed, The Cell, It Follows, Hocus Pocus*

WEDNESDAY, NOVEMBER 7TH 2018 (Woods)

Today has been a whirlwind. Variety announced that we were selected to be one of their annual 10 Screenwriters to Watch which is incredibly exciting. The other 9 writers are on a different level than us. We are such huge fans. They are flying all of us up to Canada to participate in the Whistler Film Festival.

Even crazier than all that, we got to meet Sam Raimi today! We told him that we've been ripping him off for years. He must hear that ten times a day. They are excited for us to write & direct an episode of *50 States of Fright*, Raimi's new anthology series. The opportunity to tell a scary story set in our home state of Iowa is something we would pay to be a part of.

Saw Jason Reitman's *The Frontrunner* yesterday to celebrate election night, ha.

Recently watched: *The Frontrunner, The Devil Wears Prada, The Trouble with Harry (no audio), Jurassic World: Fallen Kingdom, I Heart Huckabees, The Haunting of Hill House*

FRIDAY, NOVEMBER 16TH 2018 (Beck)

Holy shit. Just found out through a series of tweets, texts, and emails that Paul Thomas Anderson will be hosting a tastemaker's screening/event for *A Quiet Place* in two weeks!!!!! This might be the most full-circle moment of this ride, considering I first met PTA at a *Boogie Nights* 20th Anniversary screening when I had just moved out to LA. Now I'm about to leave LA, and I (potentially) could meet him as a now-working screenwriter. I'm geeking out so much right now.

Also, I move to Iowa in a month. I'm getting more nervous and stressed by the day... is this the right choice? Literally just remembered that Eli Roth was sitting in front of me at that *Boogie Nights* screening in 2007. What a difference a decade makes.

Recently Watched: *Suspiria ('18), Spirited Away, The Grinch ('18), Salesman ('69), Suspicion ('41), First Reformed*

TUESDAY, NOVEMBER 27TH 2018 (Beck)

In about an hour, I'll be arriving at the Paul Thomas Anderson hosted *A Quiet Place* event. I'm freaking out – like I don't want to embarrass myself in front of a hero. To make matters worse, I barely have a voice. Seems like it should be a passage out of the song "Ironic"... "you meet your childhood hero, but your voice is zero."

SIX HOURS LATER –

The night is over. Yes, we got to shake PTA's hand and tell him how he is directly responsible for *A Quiet Place*'s existence, between his introducing us to Jacques Tati films combined with wanting to one-up the first brilliant fifteen minutes of silence in *There Will Be Blood*. He commented on how beautiful it is that art can inspire in circular fashions. PTA gave an introductory speech for the night's event, conveying how he loved that the film is a B-movie executed at the highest level, which has always been our mantra! I wish I had been recording, but have a feeling my brain will continue to play this moment on loop for as long as my cells remain intact.

Other great moments: finally meeting Ethan & Erik (sound designers) to properly convey our love for their work (and vice-versa). Meeting Charlotte (the DP) to also convey our love for her work. So many talented people came together to make *A Quiet Place* what it is and it's amazing realizing how small our contribution is at the end of the day.

If tonight is the end of the road for *A Quiet Place*, then I'll give it a momentary hug, thank it for the bounties, and move ahead knowing the experience ran its course, and that course was meaningful.

Recently Watched: *A Star is Born ('18), Incredibles 2*

FRIDAY, DECEMBER 14TH 2018 (Beck)

The movers show up in about seven hours. I've been spending all my time prepping, and the gravity of this move is slowly hitting me. LA used to feel like home, but now that aura is slipping away. I walk outside and realize this is no longer my neighborhood. I don't belong here. There's sadness, but on the other hand, I think about if I WEREN'T moving...I'd most likely feel sadness for not being closer to family, and only seeing them a few times a year at most especially when my daughter is young. Maybe we'll love it in Iowa and never want to leave. I'm quickly accepting that life is fleeting and there's hardly a wrong decision you can make. And a year flies by so fast. I need to start meditating or having a moment of solitude to reflect... and to try and slow life down.

Recently Watched: *Burden of Dreams, Critters, Inside Out*

THURSDAY, FEBRUARY 21ST 2019 (Woods)
Just got horrible news.

Haunt distribution is looking dire. Feels like the market for original indie films belly flopped overnight. Several early bidders have since downgraded their theatrical commitment, and a few other low-ball offers weren't competitive enough to stick. We went through a painful exercise where a couple major studios were considering backing the film into an established franchise. Blumhouse thought about making it a *Halloween* spinoff for about five seconds. Our worst fear that this business can only sustain sequels, remakes, and pre-branded IP has come true.

After stringing us along with theatrical wide release offers for months, we are now being told the film will be a day & date release in ten markets and VOD. Worst of all, they want to change the title to add the word "HALLOWEEN" into it. A schlocky attempt to get impulse buyers to accidentally think this has something to do with the Carpenter universe.

I honestly don't know if I'm cut out for this business. Turns out we just spent three years of our lives making "HALLOWEEN HAUNT"?

Recently Watched: *Full Frontal (w/commentary), The Hateful Eight, True Detective (Season 3), In Plain Sight*

THURSDAY, FEBRUARY 28TH 2019 (Woods)
Feeling depressed today. Tried writing some opening pages on *65* but didn't land on anything too impressive. Spent most the afternoon searching for fonts to use in the script. Sometimes I worry we're just fucking around with fonts to get out of the actual hard work of writing.

I got 3rd place in a game of Tetris 99. So I guess there's that. Yay.......

Recently Watched: *The Possession of Hannah Grace, The Guilty, The Masked Singer, Shark Tank (an endless amount of this show)*

THURSDAY, MARCH 21ST 2019 (Beck)

Re-watched a documentary about Nicolas Winding Refn and his bankruptcy period in 2003-2004, which is not so much a "cautionary" tale as it is a "a very possible experience" tale. One major takeaway to remember, is a sentiment he shares: people always expect life to keep getting better. But I realize, there's no guarantee of that. You could suffer a personal loss tomorrow, or a slow decline, or a health issue, or watch your career fade. There's not a specific lesson to learn that can guide you forward better, rather than a reminder that you should take your peace while you can.

Recently Watched: *Sons and Daughters of Thunder, Can You Ever Forgive Me?, Gambler ('06)*

TUESDAY, APRIL 30TH 2019 (Beck)

Today was one of those days where I feel like a fraud. I'm juggling so many different projects (including life) that I just can't seem to make a substantial dent in any creative endeavor.

I've been wearing my producer hat recently, which is not glamourous. I'm learning so much about what it's like to be on the other side of the table and listening to writers pitch their takes. The process reminds me so much of casting, in that it's disheartening to see someone put forth effort into a take, only to have it quickly discarded once they leave the room. But in this case, it's even worse, given that writers have to re-read scripts several times and meticulously prepare a take on the material.

Recently Watched: *White Boy Rick, School of Rock, Birdman*

SUNDAY, JUNE 2ND 2019 (Beck)

Haunt is going to be released Friday the 13th in September.[22] We had a productive conversation last week about marketing, and just got invited to premiere as the opening night film at the Popcorn Frights

---

[22] Thankfully all conversations about adding the word "Halloween" to the title were eventually dropped.

festival in Miami this August. Excited to get our film family back together and enjoy the release.

Recently Watched: *First Man, Behind the Candelabra*

THURSDAY, JULY 10TH 2019 **(Beck)**
Haunt is making its international premiere end of next month at FrightFest. Bryan discovered this news via a Deadline Hollywood announcement of the lineup. I honestly thought the festival had already released their picks and we had no chance. So when Bryan texted me the info, I was fucking excited. Plus – PLUS – *Haunt* is screening at the Prince Charles Cinema, which is a theater I distinctly remember from my 2015 London trip. Christy and I walked past it, and I thought the theater looked like a cinephile's dream.

Recently Watched: *Ralph Breaks the Internet, Midsommar*

SATURDAY, JULY 27TH 2019 **(Woods)**
Saw Tarantino's latest film at the Hollywood Arclight. The movie accomplished something that I thought was impossible. It made me beam with pride that I live in Los Angeles and work in the movie business. Tarantino is one of the great inspirations of my life. So grateful for every film we get of his. He has not made a bad movie. We've made several.

Recently Watched: *Once Upon A Time… in Hollywood, I Wanna Hold Your Hand, I Trapped the Devil, When Jeff Tries to Save the World, Iconoclasts: Tarantino/Apple, Nightmare Cinema*

FRIDAY, AUGUST 2ND 2019 **(Woods)**
Haunt premieres in one week. So scared. Scared no one will turn up for the screening. Scared the critics are going to eviscerate us a month before our release date, before we even get out of the gate. Scared we'll be too stressed to have fun. Scared. Scared. Scared.

Recently Watched: *Haunt (recorded DVD commentary!) Escape Room, Terrifier, Solaris (w/commentary), Black Mirror: USS Callister*

TUESDAY, AUGUST 6TH 2019 **(Beck)**

Today marks the 20th anniversary of *The Sixth Sense*. So we tweeted about it with this:

Beck/Woods ☑
@beckandwoods   ...

Twenty years ago today, @MNightShyamalan redefined our love of cinema with #TheSixthSense. Enjoy this forum post from the year 2000, written by an adorable 16-year-old Bryan Woods....

Bryan Woods' post on an M. Night Shyamalan fan forum, circa 2000

Hello Mr. Shyamalan. My name is Bryan Woods and I started writing screenplays when I was fourteen.

On august 6 of 1999 I saw a movie called the Sixth Sense. It changed the way I looked at movies forever. I realized that movies can be just as smart as books and much more smart when created as brilliantly as you had created The Sixth Sense and Unbreakable. I as a screenwriter have realized a few very important things. Things I learned from Shyamalan. I learned that originality is extremely important. I learned that when writing a script I should make sure that the story needs to be told in form of a movie. Like how Unbreakable and The Sixth Sense needed to be seen rather than read because of the many visual clues that Shyamalan uses. Thankyou Night for everything you have taught me.

I am now 16 years old and I have written two full length screenplays. My friends and I also make short films that I both write and direct. Our website is www.imagineworks.8m.com

I don't know that Shyamalan will actually ever read this but it sounded like, from many of the posts above, that he might. So if you ever read this send me an email at ███████@aol.com Even if it is just to say hi. Thanks again for creating two of my most favorite movies. Thankyou for being so damn brilliant!!! Thankyou for teaching me so much!!!

8:32 AM · Aug 6, 2019 · Twitter Web App

And not even two hours later, Shyamalan tweeted us back:

M. Night Shyamalan
@MNightShyamalan

···

I just tried your AOL account. It's not going through. So I'll send my reply to you here. Thank you for your incredible generosity. To know you were inspired by something I made is touching. Know you inspired me right back. Continued success and happiness.

Ho. Ly. Sh. It.

Recently Watched: *Inglourious Basterds, Once Upon A Time… in Hollywood*

MONDAY, AUGUST 12ᵀᴴ, 2019 (Beck)

I'm officially on the other side of the *Haunt* premiere and couldn't be more relieved by the response.

The entire experience was way beyond any expectations I set… and while those expectations were super low, the reality went way way way way way fucking beyond what I had hoped. The movie sent electricity throughout the audience, and I could feel every moment through them, whether it's the suspense, comedy, horror, or relief. The love I have for the festival organizers (all volunteering their time!!!!) is impossible to express.

If the remainder of the *Haunt* release is downhill, I can rest easy having had this experience.

Recently Watched: *Once Upon A Time… in Hollywood, Nashville*

WEDNESDAY, AUGUST 13ᵀᴴ 2019 (Beck)

First review surfaced for *Haunt*. It's negative. They thought the characters lacked depth and the plot was predictable and basic.

SATURDAY, SEPTEMBER 7TH 2019 (Beck)

The Los Angeles Premiere of *Haunt* is in two hours.[23] I feel nothing.

Maybe it's peace with what the movie is. Maybe it's nerves that won't surface for another two hours. Maybe it's the acceptance of both the good and bad reviews we have already received and being able to accept both sides of the spectrum and understand each point of view, as I share most of their opinions. Maybe it's because I'm focused on the next project. Maybe it's my age. Maybe it's my aspiration to have lower blood pressure. Or maybe it's because I got to make a movie.

And that's the reward in and of itself. Because the audience response won't bring me more happiness than that which I can find in myself during the rest of the filmmaking process or better yet, life itself.

Recently Watched: *Somewhere, Triple Frontier, Long Shot*

MONDAY, SEPTEMBER 9TH 2019 (Beck)

The *Haunt* premiere was pretty fucking fun.

It wasn't filled to capacity, but it felt like it, given the lively reactions throughout the film. People dug it. There was a technical fuckup with the film playing in the wrong aspect ratio, which meant they tried to fix it, fucked it up more, we complained, they went to restart the movie, and then everyone rewatched the first 6 minutes again. That was lame, but I don't think it affected anyone's viewing by the end.

The only downside of these events, is the sheer amount of friends and family that I don't get to talk to in depth. There are so many people I love and wish to catch up with, but, like a wedding, you're lucky if you get five superficial minutes together.

Recently Watched: *L.A. Story, Good Boys*

---

[23] The Los Angeles premiere of *Haunt* was hosted at the legendary Egyptian Theatre in Hollywood, California. Eli Roth moderated a Q&A after the screening.

FRIDAY, SEPTEMBER 13TH 2019 (Beck)

These last 36 hours have been surreal. Bryan & I have/will be spending four days in different cities – Vancouver/Los Angeles/Quad Cities/back to Vancouver.

We're at LAX, about to board a red-eye to Iowa to premiere *Haunt* to our hometown crowd in our hometown theater where we premiered our features as 20-year-olds. And actually, *Haunt* was released today, and we got rave reviews from the LA Times, Richard Roeper, and The Hollywood Reporter, which I never fucking expected. Not that I live by the Tomato-meter, but it's nice that it's a tomato and not a splat.

Recently Watched: *8 Million Ways to Die, Jaws, It Chapter Two*

Speaking with Eli Roth (far left) at the *Haunt* premiere, held at the Egyptian Theatre in Hollywood.

SUNDAY, SEPTEMBER 22ND 2019 (Woods)

Been following all the *Haunt* reactions on Twitter, Instagram, etc. It's been really gratifying to see how much fun people are having with the film. It belongs to the audience now, so it's time to turn our attention to the next project.

I'm writing this from the Denver airport, heading to Vancouver to direct an episode of *50 States of Fright* with Sam Raimi. We have just closed Taissa Farmiga as the lead for Hannah. And just got the glorious news that Ron Livingston is going to be our Blake. Fucking dream cast WOW.

The show will premiere on Quibi, an app where you watch content exclusively on your phone. People think this platform is going to be the next big thing. We'll see!

POSTLUDE

...Quibi was *not* the next big thing. In actual fact, outside of our family and a few friends, we're not sure anyone even saw our episode of *50 States of Fright* when it aired September 28, 2020, two months before Jeffrey Katzenberg's platform went dark. But that's what makes our Quibi chapter such a perfect case study for being a professional in the film business. That show lead to us meeting Sam Raimi and having a great experience working together. Which then lead to him producing our next film *65*, starring Adam Driver which, at the time of this book's publication, comes out in 2023. You never know where each project will take you. Of course, we wish more people experienced *50 States* because we are immensely proud of the work, but we'll take the consolation prize. See what we mean about highs and lows?

You learn to be grateful for every setback. No one has it all figured out. If filmmakers and studios could predict what was going to work and what wasn't, they would never produce a failure ever again. So maybe the key is to keep your antenna out, follow your heart, and always be ready to go where the wind blows you. It is a privilege – both exciting and terrifying – to be able to pursue a creative endeavor that we love, and to be able to put work into the world for others to experience. In the case of *Haunt*, we must acknowledge the contributions of our collaborators who helped make it happen.

Thank you to our producers Todd Garner, Jeremy Stein, and Mark Fasano for bringing us all together on this wicked journey. Gratitude to Eli Roth for his mentorship, and for supporting the movie all the way through to release. Love to our cast, both the heroes and the monsters, for making this story their own. Admiration to our crew who worked tirelessly bringing this film to life (we hope our journals illuminate how hard your jobs really were on this one). Respect to the wonderful folks at Sierra/Affinity and eOne for taking a chance on us, and for letting our team blur the line between art and entertainment. We could not have done any of this without the uncompromising love and support of our families and friends. And most importantly, thank you to all of the fans who have helped keep this movie alive beyond its initial release. You have blown away every humble expectation we ever had to the point of incomprehension.

After all the dust cleared, *Haunt* debuted on the streaming service Shudder as the #1 most watched movie of 2019. We were fortunate the film garnered some support in the critical community, where it placed on over a dozen year-end "best of" lists for achievement in horror. To our endless fascination, the film has spawned no less than four incredible t-shirt lines and counting, as well as a series of officially licensed Halloween costumes, action figures, special edition Blu-rays, soundtracks, and more. And when the film was included on an episode of Job Bob Brigg's *The Last Drive-in* – as longtime fans of *MonsterVision* – our faces had finally melted to the floor. Thank you all from the bottom of our heart.

Flipping back through our journals in anticipation of this release, we noticed a theme start to materialize. In the aftermath of *Haunt* and *A Quiet Place*, we realized there is no reward at the end of the process that is more fulfilling (or for that matter more *FUN!*), than the act of creating the work itself. In other words: the work is the reward. Which is a thrilling concept we wish we understood earlier in life. It illustrates a beautiful notion that whether you're a seasoned professional, or an amateur filmmaker roughing it with an iPhone and some friends, there is nothing stopping you from living your dreams right now. Go make your movie. Anything that happens after that is up to the wind.

SCREENPLAY

SCREENPLAY INTRODUCTION

The following screenplay is presented in its original format, with colored text, justified slugs, and font play.

There are so many things we wish we could change about this screenplay. Story decisions we made that upon reflection feel a little forced or too easy. Lines of dialogue that are almost baffling with a bit of perspective. Who talks like that? Worse, who *writes* like that? And the scene descriptions! This script contains some writing that would embarrass even the most amateur scribe. And of course, there are always the compromises... the compromises we shouldn't have made, and even more regrettable, the compromises we *should* have made, but were too blinded by our own vision to see it.

This script is a time-capsule of where we were as writers in the summer of 2016, warts and all. But we also hope it captures how much fun we had writing it. Because if nothing else, it was a hell of a lot of fun to write.

Beck/Woods

71

HAUNT

by
Scott Beck & Bryan Woods

Eli Roth
Sierra/Affinity
Broken Road Productions
Nickel City Pictures

EXT. UNIVERSITY HOUSING - SUNSET

A college neighborhood in the fall.

TRACKING along porches filled with JACK-O-LANTERNS. Dozens of
carved PUMPKINS. Every doorstep in this housing tract adorned
with festive decorations anticipating Halloween. **Except one.**

HOLD on the empty porch of a TWO-STORY college house.

No decorations. No holiday pumpkins carved with care. Just a
barren mahogany door. Something ominous about it...

SMASH!! -- A PUMPKIN EXPLODES AGAINST THE DOOR -- SLAM TO:

INT. TWO-STORY, BEDROOM - SUNSET

HARPER (20) looks out the second story window, shaken. Her
girl-next-door face marred by a day old BRUISE under her eye.

Harper grabs her phone. The lock-screen is a photo of her
boyfriend **SAM** (22), posing next to his RED PICKUP. Sam's
ordinary features hide a complicated and dangerous anger.

Harper's hands tremble as she drafts a TEXT to him:

> **I'M SORRY**

Her thumb hovers over SEND. Thinking. Unsure. Afraid...

A KNOCK AT THE DOOR.

> HARPER
> Yeah?

> BAILEY (O.S.)
> Your door's locked.

> HARPER
> Just a sec.

Harper scrambles over to a RED COMPACT MIRROR. Dries her
eyes. Pads her swollen cheeks with concealer. Coats LAYERS OF
MAKEUP over her bruise until it's invisible.

This is a MASK Harper regularly wears... a look that says
"everything is okay". You wouldn't even know she's been
through the worst week of her life.

Harper answers the door.

                    HARPER
                (playing it cool)
            What's up?

BAILEY (21), a no nonsense senior, wears a painfully
uncreative SEXY KITTY costume. Something about her
disaffected demeanor suggests a slight air of superiority.

                    BAILEY
            Someone just fucking threw a
            pumpkin at our door.

                    HARPER
            Okay?

                    BAILEY
            Okay, so... did your boyfriend just
            throw a pumpkin at our door?

                    HARPER
            What, that's not something he'd do.

                    BAILEY
            That's exactly something he'd do.

                    MALLORY (O.S.)
                (flapper voice)
            Darling, is that what you're
            wearing?

Harper looks at her RED HOODIE, suddenly self-conscious.

                    HARPER
            For what?

MALLORY (21), theater major, flirty free-spirit, wears a
1920s FLAPPER costume and occasionally acts the part with her
rapid-fire old-timey SLANG:

                    MALLORY
                (flapper voice)
            You can't go to a costume party
            looking like a bug-eyed Betty! You
            look positively zozzled!

                    BAILEY
            Mallory, you're not going anywhere
            if you keep zozzling that goddamn
            accent.

                    MALLORY
                (flapper voice)
            Get used to it, Noodle Juice!
                (MORE)

> MALLORY (cont'd)
> Just heard I'm a lock for the
> winter production of THOROUGHLY
> MODERN MILLIE. I needs to rehearse!

> BAILEY
> (to Harper)
> We got invited to the Halloween
> party at Summit. Bunch of hot
> baseball players. Maybe you can
> meet somebody who's not a psycho.

Harper squirms, doesn't like being pressured to go out.

> HARPER
> I'm probably staying in. Sam's
> supposed to come over later and --

> BAILEY
> -- bullshit.

Bailey barges into Harper's room. She grabs her PHONE off the
desk, notices the "I'M SORRY" text Harper drafted.

> HARPER
> Don't, Bailey...

> BAILEY
> No, you're breaking up with this
> bitch tonight.

> HARPER
> Bailey, stop!

Bailey deletes "I'M SORRY" and replaces it with:

IT'S OVER

Before Bailey hits send, Harper snatches her phone back.

> HARPER
> Everything's fine.

> BAILEY
> Nothing's ever "fine" with Sam.
> He's an alcoholic Harper. You know
> how I can tell? Because he's an
> alcoholic.

> HARPER
> You barely know him.

> BAILEY
> All I'm saying is...

Bailey grabs a MOONSTONE RING from Harper's vanity.

                    BAILEY
          ...I came to your room last night
          to steal some jewelry for my
          costume, and you were passed out...

Bailey slips the MOONSTONE RING onto her finger.

                    HARPER
          Careful, that's my mom's.

                    BAILEY
          ...Harper, you had a bruise on your
          face.

Bailey heads for the door, pauses.

                    BAILEY
          If your psycho boyfriend ever comes
          back, I'm calling the fucking cops.

Bailey leaves. There's clearly history between these two.

                    HARPER
          Do you _see_ a bruise!

That mild whimper is about as defiant as Harper gets.

                    ANGELA (O.S.)
               (sorry, but...)
          There's minor swelling, indicating
          a contusion on the orbital plate.

ANGELA (20), a premed student who's dressed like a ZOMBIE
NURSE, enters the room. She's quirky, with a dry sense of
humor. Sees through Harper's attempt to hide the bruise.

                    ANGELA
          You should come out with us. Take
          your mind off the boyfriend drama.

                    HARPER
          There's no boyfriend drama...

Mallory places a comforting hand on Harper's face. Starts to
reapply MAKEUP over the bruise.

                    MALLORY
               (finally her real voice)
          60 grand a year for theater school,
          and all I've learned is stage makeup.

                    ANGELA
          Try eight years of medical school,
          surrounded by an extended family of
          prestigious doctors --

Angela struggles with a couple HAIRPINS on her costume.

                    ANGELA
          -- and you can't even fasten the
          bobby pins on your fake nurse hat.

                    HARPER
               (winces)
          Ouch.

Mallory dabs a little too hard, distracted by her phone;
obsessively refreshing the winter play's CAST LIST website.

                    MALLORY
          Sorry, they still haven't posted
          the cast list. I'm gonna be a space
          case all night.

                    ANGELA
          Harper, empirically speaking, I
          assume we live together. But
          anecdotally, you never come out
          with us. In fact, the only time
          we're conscious of your existence
          is when you cut a rent check.

                    MALLORY
          Which is due, by the way.
               (flapper voice)
          Three-hundred clams.

Mallory realizes that wasn't the right time. She grimaces an
apology and heads for the door.

                    ANGELA
          So maybe come out and have fun for
          once. It's good medicine.

                    HARPER
          I don't have a costume... it'll be
          weird.

                    ANGELA
          It's Halloween. Weird is good.

Angela walks away. Harper takes a deep breath. Looks at the
"IT'S OVER" TEXT Bailey drafted. She's thinking...

HARPER HITS **"SEND"**.

SELECTS **"BLOCK THIS NUMBER?"**.

PRESSES **"YES"**.

A weight immediately lifts off Harper's chest.

INT. VOLKSWAGEN - NIGHT

Harper rides in back of Bailey's VOLKSWAGEN PASSAT. Music bumps. Bailey controls the playlist, as always. Mallory keeps refreshing the CAST LIST. The girls all dance and sing along.

Harper rolls down the window. Feels the fall breeze in her hair, forces a smile. Starts mouthing the words to the song.

Maybe this will be a good night after all.

EXT. BAR DISTRICT - NIGHT

The VOLKSWAGEN arrives outside a lively downtown district just off campus and completely decked out for Halloween.

INT. SUMMIT, ENTRANCE - NIGHT

The girls enter The Summit, an old collegial hotspot that's been converted into a trendy arcade bar. CLUB MUSIC plays.

Everyone is in costume. EVERYONE. Well, besides Harper... who's starting to feel super out of place right now.

The girls are ushered through a queue to be judged for the bar's COSTUME CONTEST. A P.A. corners the girls.

> P.A.
> (scanning the girls)
> Costume contest? Costume contest?
> (sees Harper)
> What're you supposed to be?

> HARPER
> (deflecting glances)
> I'm dressed as a college student, ha.

People don't find it funny. It's almost offensive that she doesn't have a costume.

INT. SUMMIT, BOOTH - NIGHT

A TRAY OF DRINKS clinks down on their table.

>   MALLORY
>   (flapper voice)
>   Delish! What kind of Hooch are we
>   bootleggin'?

>   BAILEY
>   Spider Vodka.

>   MALLORY
>   (real voice)
>   Fuck you.

Suspended inside the Vodka bottle is a lifeless Huntsman
spider. This is real. Google it.

>   BAILEY
>   It's from Thailand. They put a
>   ceremonial spider in each bottle.

>   MALLORY
>   I know it's Halloween, but you
>   can't do this to me tonight.

Bailey passes out the drinks. Harper awkwardly holds hers
with two hands like a latte, clearly not a drinker.

>   BAILEY
>   You're still afraid of spiders?

>   ANGELA
>   If you're really an actor, just
>   pretend it's something else.

>   MALLORY
>   Yeah, that usually helps with
>   blowjobs.

Mallory closes her eyes and knocks back the "Spider Shot".

Their attention drifts to the COSTUME CONTEST hosted by an
M.C. A train of GIRLS IN SKIMPY LINGERIE are doing very well
with the JUDGES.

>   BAILEY
>   Cool. Did anyone else just see that
>   vagina costume win first place?

                    ANGELA
          Going commando <u>does</u> reduce your
          risk of yeast infection and UTIs.
          My cousin Lynn is a Gynecologist.

                    BAILEY
               (scanning the bar)
          Well then, there's a lot of healthy
          girls here tonight.

Bailey wrangles her friends for a SELFIE.

                    BAILEY
          Everyone say, "Happy HO-lloween!"

She snaps the pic and starts uploading it to INSTAGRAM but
gets distracted --

                    BAILEY
               -- Nathan!

Bailey runs over to **NATHAN** (22), a charismatic athlete in
great shape, who phoned it in this Halloween with a BASEBALL
BAT, HELMET, and JERSEY from the Southern Illinois University
team, which he plays for.

                    NATHAN
          Hey there. Worried you guys weren't
          gonna make it.

Bailey gives Nathan an overly affectionate hug that makes him
a little uncomfortable. They have an on-again off-again
dynamic. Nathan can never really tell when Bailey's into him.

                    NATHAN
          Was it hard to find us? This place
          is crazy tonight --

                    BAILEY
               (attention elsewhere)
          Ty Hoffman!!

Bailey nudges past Nathan and heads over to **TY HOFFMAN** (21),
the statuesque All-American first baseman for SIU and the
reason Nathan has been riding the bench all season.

                    NATHAN
          Good talk.

Now Bailey's riding Ty. See, that's what we're talking about.
Is Bailey into Nathan? Playing games? Who knows...

Harper watches Nathan from the booth. Nathan catches her
gaze, smiles.

Harper looks away, caught. Nathan waves her over.

Harper points at herself, "Me?". Nathan nods.

Harper looks left. Looks right. Blocked in on both sides by Mallory & Angela. Fuck it.

Harper crawls under the table. She approaches Nathan, who seems surprised.

                    HARPER
          Hey.

                    NATHAN
          Did you need something?

                    HARPER
          What? You were talking to my
          friend, and then waved me over.

                    NATHAN
          Me? No I was... motioning for
          another drink.

Just then, a WAITRESS hands Nathan a BEER.

Harper realizes there is a second bar right behind their booth. This is the worst moment of her life.

                    HARPER
          I'm so sorry.

                    NATHAN
               (feels bad)
          Do you know Bailey?

                    HARPER
          Yeah, we were freshmen together.

Nathan looks at Harper, thinks he recognizes her.

                    NATHAN
          You're one of her yoga students?

                    HARPER
          Roommate, actually. I'm Harper.

                    NATHAN
               (remembering)
          Sorry, yeah, I've totally heard
          about you.

                         HARPER
                      (flattered)
              Oh, yeah? What'd you hear?

                         NATHAN
                 Everything okay with your
                 boyfriend?

                         HARPER
              Oh... Yeah.

Harper frowns, definitely the worst moment of her life. Just
then, a CONFETTI CANON on the ceiling explodes. (Confetti
rains down behind their heads for the remainder of their CUs)

                         NATHAN
                 Surprised we haven't met. I never see
                 you and Bailey out together.

                         HARPER
                 I don't really get out much.

                         NATHAN
                      (totally gets it)
                 Look at my costume. Someone
                 reminded me it was Halloween five
                 minutes ago, I rolled out of bed,
                 grabbed my lucky bat, and showed up
                 like this. I hate these things.

Harper smiles, didn't expect the kindness.

                         HARPER
                 At least you have a costume.

                         NATHAN
                 What are you talking about? You
                 have a dope costume.

Harper isn't sure if he's joking. Nathan reaches behind
Harper's head and pulls the hood up on her red hoodie.

                         NATHAN
                 Little Red Riding Hood. It's
                 perfect.

Harper laughs, RIGHT AS --

                         EVAN (O.S.)
                 BULLSHIT!!

-- BEER GETS SPLASHED IN HER FACE.

                    NATHAN
            Evan, what the fuck?!

EVAN (22), the last of our group, is a nerdy shapeless try-
hard, who's a bit confrontational, hates authority. He just
knocked a row of drinks off a PINBALL MACHINE.

                    EVAN
              (losing his shit)
            I can't believe it!

Evan's wearing a BROWN SACK with TENTACLES and ANTENNAS
protruding from different areas of his body. It's a little
abstract, as if striving for some grand vision that falls way
short - a metaphor in many ways for Evan's life.

Nathan grabs some napkins for Harper, while Mallory & Angela
approach.

                    NATHAN
              (to Evan)
            What are you supposed to be?

                    EVAN
            I'm the front half of a Human
            Centipede. The other two guys just
            bailed. Now I'm gonna look like a
            total jackass!

                    MALLORY
            Now you're gonna look like a
            jackass?

Angela examines a compartment on Evan's butt where the rest
of the costume presumably connects.

                    ANGELA
            Did they bail because they didn't
            want to eat ass all night?

                    EVAN
            No, they probably bailed because
            this bar sucks! These machines keep
            jacking my quarters! I'm over here
            spending a goddamn fortune on
            Frogger like it's 1981.

                    ANGELA
            I think they were just fucking with
            you, dude.

                    EVAN
            Oberhaus and KFC said they were
            coming.

                         ANGELA
                       (pointing)
              Oberhaus and KFC are right over
              there with the rest of the team.

Sure enough, Oberhaus and KFC are dressed as MUSTARD and
KETCHUP, playing dizzy bat with the others.

                         EVAN
                    (under his breath)
              Motherfuckers.

                         ANGELA
              No one wants to be the ass end of a
              human centipede.

Evan gets right in Angela's face, like he's ready to start a
fight, but instead --

                         EVAN
              Fuck this shit-show.

-- reaches under Angela's NURSE HAT and plucks two HAIRPINS.
He takes the pins to a LOCKED PANEL on the PINBALL MACHINE.

                         EVAN
              I'm getting a refund.

Evan strips the rubber tip off one pin, and bends the other
into a right angle, fashioning them into a LOCK PICK KIT.

                         ANGELA
              Are you seriously lock picking that
              pinball machine?

                         EVAN
              I can lock pick anything. Like that
              diary under Mallory's mattress.

                         MALLORY
                       (distracted)
              What?

Mallory isn't listening. She refreshes the CAST LIST website
again. And again. And again.

                         EVAN
              Happy Halloween, motherfuckers.

CLICK! The pinball panel swings open. QUARTERS start spilling
everywhere, like a slot machine jackpot.

Ty and Bailey make their way back to the group. Ty notices
Evan scooping the growing mass of coins into his costume.

                         TY
              Whoa, whoa! You're gonna get the
              whole team kicked out.

                         EVAN
              What're you talking about, they let
              us do whatever we want. We own this
              place.

                         TY
              We? You're not on the team. You're
              just the equipment manager.

                         EVAN
              I could walk onto this team in my
              fucking sleep.

He could not walk onto this team in a million years.

                         TY
              You need to dial it down.

                         EVAN
              Dial it down?! I only have one
              setting and that's 11. You don't
              want to see me go to 12.

Ty towers over Evan. David meet Goliath.

                         TY
              Either dial it down, or we can take
              it outside, Bruh.

                         EVAN
              Don't call me Bruh, BITCH.

                         TY
              Bailey if this clown's with you,
              you're all gonna have to bounce.

                         BAILEY
                    (flirty)
              Ty... think you could make an
              exception just this once?

Ty starts motioning for security. Bailey stops him, wraps her
arm around Harper --

                         BAILEY
              Harper here has had an awful night.
              And she only had two requests to
              make everything better. The first,
              being a night out with her friends.

                    TY
          And the second?

                  BAILEY
          To meet SIU's star baseball player.

Nathan rolls his eyes as Harper buries her head with
embarrassment.

                    TY
               (to Harper)
          That so?

Harper lifts her gaze to Ty, who smiles back. They lock eyes
for a moment. Ty's smile fades. His eyes narrow. Something's
wrong...

Harper suddenly realizes HER BRUISE IS VISIBLE. The make-up
has faded from the drink Evan spilled on her.

INT. SUMMIT, RESTROOM - NIGHT

Harper stands in the restroom, alone. She uses her RED
COMPACT MIRROR to reapply MAKE-UP over the bruise.

A KNOCK ON THE DOOR.

                  HARPER
          Occupied.

Harper checks her PHONE. Notices a new notification: "SAM
LIKED A PHOTO YOU WERE TAGGED IN". Harper clicks on the photo
and *FUCK*, it's the selfie she took with the girls. Bailey GEO-
TAGGED the location. Now Sam knows where she is.

ANOTHER LOUD KNOCK.

                  HARPER
          One second.

Harper opens the door... NO ONE IS THERE.

EXT. SUMMIT, ALLEY - NIGHT

Harper steps outside into an alley behind The Summit. An
EMPLOYEE snuffs out a cigarette and exits.

She pulls up Google Maps on her PHONE. Types in "MOM'S
HOUSE". Street View loads an image of a quaint SUBURBAN HOME.

She clicks "recommended route", distance: 22 MINUTES BY CAR.
She tabs over to "walking distance": 65 MINUTES BY FOOT.

A DOOR SLAMS. Harper turns, startled.

                    NATHAN
          Saw you heading towards the exit.
          Got worried you left.

Nathan lifts a GIANT BAG of HALLOWEEN CANDY.

                    NATHAN
          The team awarded me worst costume.
          Figured I'd share it with the
          runner-up.

Nathan offers her a SNICKERS. Harper smiles, takes the candy.

                    NATHAN
          Know any good ghost stories?

                    HARPER
          Ghost stories?

                    NATHAN
          That's what people do on Halloween,
          right? Tell each other scary
          stories so no matter how shitty
          your life is, it seems great
          compared to the person in the
          story. I'll go first.

Harper laughs.

                    NATHAN
          This one's true: When I was eleven,
          we came home from vacation, and our
          front door was broken wide open. My
          dad enters the house, like he's
          Liam Neeson or something, while my
          mom and I wait outside. I'm frozen.
          Heart's beating a mile a minute.
          Too afraid to go inside. And I look
          up to my room, which was on the
          second story, and I see a light
          turn on. A few moments pass, my dad
          comes back outside. I say, "Was
          there anyone in my room?" and he
          looks at me with this face that
          I'll never forget. I start to get
          afraid when I realize how afraid he
          is. He tells me, "I didn't check
          your room." We all look up to the
          second story window and say, "Then
          who turned on the light?".
               (beat)
          The police eventually come.
                    (MORE)

NATHAN (cont'd)
They don't find anyone in the
house. For the rest of my life, I
was too scared to sleep in that
room.

HARPER
Maybe the light was already on when
you got there, and you just forgot?

NATHAN
(smiles, nods)
Well yeah, but that's not a good
scary story. How about you?

HARPER
Um, me? So like scary stories from
when I was young? So. I don't know.

FLASH CUT: *Harper's childhood home. Midwest suburbia. White
picket fence. American Flag on the porch.*

NATHAN
Nothing scary ever happened to you?

HARPER
(thinking)
Scary? Okay... scary... hmm...

FLASH CUT: *Young Harper hiding under her bed, her face red
from crying.*

HARPER
No, I mean, my parents were really
great and everything. We have a
good relationship. *Had* a good
relationship. Everything was great.

Nathan realizes he touched a nerve, decides to back off.

NATHAN
Yeah, I don't talk to my parents
either.

Harper glances back at Google Maps, considering the walk. The
Street View of her childhood home is overtaken by an incoming
TEXT from an anonymous number:

GUESS MY COSTUME?

She looks ahead, nervous. There's a large pedestrian mall in
the distance, where dozens of COSTUMED STUDENTS walk by.

NATHAN
Harper?

Harper sees someone wearing a DEVIL **MASK** over a HOODED ROBE, heading this way. For a moment they lock eyes. Is it Sam?

The Devil stops. Hangs a FLYER. Then disappears into the crowd

Harper takes a deep breath.

> HARPER
> I think I should go.

> NATHAN
> I think you should stay.
> (beat)
> Halloween is all about the power of pretending. Let's both <u>pretend</u> we're having the best night ever. We laugh harder than the others. We dance more. We play the shit out of some Jenga. Harper, I promise to pretend you're gonna have a fun night.

> HARPER
> (shakes her head)
> Maybe just a little longer.

BEGIN MONTAGE:

Nathan and Harper rejoin the group. They root for an intoxicated Angela as she decimates a karaoke track. They joke about Evan's unorthodox dance moves. They <u>laugh harder,</u> <u>dance more</u>, and have an amazing <u>game of oversized Jenga</u>. But are they <u>pretending</u>? Or is a delicate connection forming...

If these moments feel poignant, it's because they feel real. This sequence is Richard Linklater's DAZED & CONFUSED / EVERYBODY WANTS SOME - authentic human moments, some staged, some improvised.

INT. SUMMIT, LOUNGE - NIGHT

A little later. The group is crammed inside a VIP lounge. Harper stares at the "GUESS MY COSTUME" TEXT from earlier. She shakes off the paranoia, types a response --

> **SAM?**

-- then turns her attention back to the group.

> EVAN
> Mr. Conway?

                    BAILEY
          Decent manscaping. Fair upper-body
          strength. Disappointing erection.

                    HARPER
          What are you guys doing?

                    BAILEY
          Filling out RateMyProfessors.com
          for every teacher I've slept with.

Harper blushes. She turns to Nathan, the <u>conversation splits</u>.

              EVAN   HARPER
    How would you rate his   (to Nathan)
    "easiness"?   Is it true what they say
                                       about you?

              BAILEY   NATHAN
    Uh, I'd say pretty desperate.   What do they say?

              EVAN   HARPER
       (typing)   That you hit a five hundred
    'Kay, 5 out of 5.   footer over the right field
       (reading phone)   wall. Is it still a school
    What about his "helpfulness?"   record?

              BAILEY   NATHAN
    Could use more enthusiasm, to   Got the bat right here.
    be honest. I need motivation   (shows his bat)
    when I'm going down on a guy.   Didn't think you were the
    Some "good jobs" or "great   type who followed sports.
    work" to keep me engaged.

              EVAN   HARPER
    'Kay, 2 out of 5, for a   Stalked you on Twitter.
    combined passing grade of D+.   @HomeRunKilla12 says you
                                     could go pro.

                    EVAN
          (then across to Harper)
          Yeah, I mean, we all <u>could</u> go pro.
          But the reality is - Ty Hoffman's
          an all-around better slugger than
          Nathan. <u>That's</u> why Nathan got
          benched this season. You can't
          compete with 19 homers, 26 doubles
          and a 91 RBI. He's Nathan 2.0.

Nathan takes the abuse. No one seems to notice how much this
hurts him... except Harper.

                    HARPER
          I just think it's cool you play on
          the team.

                    EVAN
          Harper, weren't you listening? He
          doesn't even play.

INT. SUMMIT, LOFT - NIGHT

Later. Nathan leans against a POOL TABLE. He's in his own
world. Looks sad. Lines up a shot. Notices a PRESENCE --

                    NATHAN
          They still talking behind my back?

                    HARPER
          Evan's just jealous.

                    NATHAN
          The fucked up thing is, he's right.
          Last season, I took a wild pitch to
          the face. Shattered my cheekbone in
          three places. Took a year to recover.

Now that he mentions it, Harper does notice some light
scarring above Nathan's eye.

                    NATHAN
          Ever since, my swings are too
          conservative. I never lean into the
          ball for the big hits. I'm too
          afraid. They don't throw you a
          parade in baseball for hitting line
          drives. It's not sexy.

BAM! Nathan accidentally strikes the 8-ball into a pocket.

                    NATHAN
          And apparently I also suck at pool.

                    HARPER
                (smiles)
          Or you've had too much to drink.

                    NATHAN
          Or not enough. Spider Vodka?

He hands Harper the CUE.

                    NATHAN
          I'm solids, you're stripes.

She watches Nathan disappear downstairs to grab a drink. Her
phone buzzes with another TEXT from the anonymous number:

GUESS MY COSTUME?

An attachment loads. It's a picture of SOMEONE'S FACE
partially obscured by a BLURRY COSTUME.

I'LL HUFF

Harper glances around the bar, alone and vulnerable.

AND I'LL PUFF

So many different costumes, but none that quite look like
this person. Or do they? Harper zips up her red hoodie, tries
to hide her face.

AND I'LL...

A HAND CIRCLES HER WAIST.

                    VOICE (O.S.)
                  (whispers)
            ...found you.

CLOSE ON HARPER'S FACE AS ALL SOUND FADES AROUND HER. AS HER
HEART BEGINS TO POUND AGAINST HER CHEST. AS SHE TURNS AROUND.

It's not Sam. It's Ty Hoffman. Uncomfortably close.

                    HARPER
            Sorry, thought you were someone
            else.

                    TY
            Is it true?

DING! A final text comes through:

BLOW YOUR HOUSE DOWN.

                    TY
            That you're a fan of my work?

                    HARPER
            Oh, I'm alright, um.

Ty is several drinks deep, he's not hearing great right now.

                    TY
            I always make time for my fans.

                    HARPER
          Sorry, Bailey was just messing with
          me. I'm good.

Ty is not used to hearing "no".

                    TY
          Let's get a drink.

                    HARPER
          That's okay...

Ty's face darkens.

                    TY
          What'd you say?

                    NATHAN (O.S.)
          She said back off.

Nathan pushes Ty back.

                    TY
          Wasn't talking to you. I'll let you
          know if I need a pinch hitter.

Nathan avoids the confrontation, begins to usher Harper away.

                    TY
               (to Harper)
          You'd rather go home with a guy who
          can't even get to first base?

They keep walking.

                    TY
               (to Harper)
          Is he the one who fucked up your
          face?

Nathan stops. Turns around. Gets right in Ty's face.

                    TY
          You wanna do something?

Ty makes a small, quick move in Nathan's direction, like he
might hit him. <u>Nathan flinches</u>.

                    TY
          Still afraid to get hit? Take off
          that fucking jersey. You don't
          deserve it.

EXT. SUMMIT, STREET - LATER THAT NIGHT

Our group leaves the bar, heading for their cars. Mallory
tabs over to the CAST LIST website, still no results.

                    MALLORY
                (googling)
          What's next? Think the Haunted Corn
          Maze is open late. I know the cast.

                    ANGELA
          Nah, that place is a breeding
          ground for parasites.
                (yawns)
          My cousin Kim is a health
          inspector, she gave it a "D".

                    BAILEY
                (thinking)
          Uh, we could hit the food trucks on
          campus, Netflix a scary movie...

Evan rips a FLYER off the wall.

                    EVAN
          Anyone down for an extreme haunted
          house?

                    ANGELA
          Skeptical how "extreme" it's going
          to be if they're using flyers to
          advertise.

Bailey approaches the driver's side of her VOLKSWAGEN. She
stops. Her face pales. Eyes trained on the pavement.

                    NATHAN
                (noticing her)
          Bailey?

                    BAILEY
          Who the fuck would do this...

Nathan kneels. Sees the Volkswagen's TIRES HAVE BEEN SLASHED.

                    NATHAN
          ...weird.

                    BAILEY
          Now what? How am I supposed to get
          home?

                    EVAN
          Everyone can squeeze in my --

                         BAILEY
          -- we're not all gonna fit in your
          fucking Fiesta, Evan! I need my
          car! I teach yoga in the morning!

Evan reacts, *"Jesus, sorry!"*

                         NATHAN
          Could be some asshole from the
          team. Better to come back when
          everyone's sober.

Bailey paces. Feels a migraine coming on. It's getting late.

                         BAILEY
          What do you think, Harper?

Harper doesn't say anything. She doesn't think it was someone
from the team. No. She thinks it was someone else entirely.

                         HARPER
                       (softly)
          Probably better to leave.

EXT. HIGHWAY ROAD - NIGHT

A packed '96 FORD FIESTA travels an empty highway.

INT. FIESTA - NIGHT

It's loud and cramped inside. Everyone wrestles for room to
breathe as they consult their PHONES.

                         BAILEY
                       (googling)
          There's at least five haunts in the
          area. Someone just pick so we can
          call it a night.

Evan switches on a neon pink LYFT AMP on the dash.

                         NATHAN
          What're you doing?

                         EVAN
          Paying my tuition.
                       (to everyone)
          Mint? Bottled water?

Nathan notices the mini-bottled water and mints in the center
console, realizes Evan's a LYFT driver.

                         NATHAN
              What is this?

                         EVAN
              Desani flat and Cinnamon Altoids.

                         NATHAN
              No I'm saying, if you think we're
              paying you to drive us to a haunted
              house that you want to go to...

                         EVAN
              As a professional, this puts me in
              an awkward position. If I give you
              guys free rides just because we're
              friends, would it really be fair to
              my other customers?

Nathan rips the AMP off the dash. Rolls down the window.
Tosses it out --

                         EVAN
              It took me 250 rides to earn that!!

HEADLIGHTS come through the back window, Harper squints.

                         ANGELA
                    (background)
              There's a Jaycees passed the mill.

                         MALLORY
                    (background)
              Wow, we're really settling.

Harper watches the rearview. Holding her breath. The
HEADLIGHTS reach the intersection behind them.

Evan takes a left. The truck behind them does too. Harper,
mind racing...

                         HARPER
              Evan, can you turn up here. I know
              a shortcut to the mill.

EXT. HIGHWAY ROAD, FORK - NIGHT

The Fiesta slows to a fork in the road. Turns right.

INT. FIESTA - NIGHT

Nathan notices the detour, leans over to Evan.

                    NATHAN
          Where are we going?

                    EVAN
          Yeah, Harper, where are we going?

Harper swallows. Isn't sure how to say this. Doesn't want to
sound crazy.

                    HARPER
               (low)
          Someone's following us.

The girls continue their conversation in the back, oblivious.

                    MALLORY
               (background)
          Isn't there like a Haunted House at
          the hospital tonight?

                    ANGELA
               (background)
          I can't show my face at the
          hospital with my grades.

THE HEADLIGHTS REAPPEAR, GAINING MOMENTUM.

THIS TIME EVAN AND NATHAN NOTICE.

HARPER CAN'T BELIEVE IT.

AN AWFUL MINUTE.

AS IT FOLLOWS.

EVAN SPEEDS UP. TURNS A SHARP CORNER. LOSES THE HEADLIGHTS.

EXT. FOREST ROAD - NIGHT

The Fiesta pulls over to the shoulder. The engine and lights
turn off. A silent moment passes.

INT. FIESTA - SHOULDER OF THE ROAD - NIGHT

Everyone looks up from their phones, wonder why Evan stopped.

                    BAILEY
          What's going on?

                    EVAN
          Harper thinks we're being stalked.

                         HARPER
              No, it's just... did anyone see a
              truck follow us from the bar?

Harper stares out the back window into a dark void, waiting
for the headlights...

The others turn around, one by one, looking into the dark,
waiting for the truck to emerge, and JUST THEN --

BZZZZZZPT - A BRIGHT NEON SIGN ILLUMINATES DOWN THE ROAD.

                         NATHAN
              What's that?

They can't quite make it out. Evan reverses, getting closer.
Half of the sign is burned out, leaving only the FIRST SIX
LETTERS visible, big and bold, coming into focus:

HAUNTED HOUSE

And as they get even closer, we see a GRAVEL PATHWAY that
leads to a large STRUCTURE in the distance.

                         EVAN
              This cannot be ignored.

Evan turns down the pathway.

                         BAILEY
              Seriously?

INT. FIESTA - PATHWAY TO HAUNTED HOUSE - NIGHT

They pass under a faded sign post, adorned with FAKE COBWEBS
and BLACK/ORANGE STREAMERS. It looks like the entrance to an
AMUSEMENT RIDE - a HAUNTED HOUSE, to be specific. The kind of
attraction that pops up in the fall, as Halloween grows near.

INT. FIESTA - PARKING LOT TO HAUNTED HOUSE - NIGHT

The Fiesta parks at the **HAUNTED HOUSE;** an ABANDONED WAREHOUSE
surrounded by a tall PERIMETER FENCE lined with barbed wire.
A few other cars are in the parking lot.

It's dark. Very dark, actually. All the lights are off except
for a single bulb illuminating the ENTRANCE.

                    ANGELA
          I think it's the haunt from Evan's
          flyer.
               (to Evan)
          If this place sucks, it's on you.

                    BAILEY
          Guys, I'm over it. We had a fun
          night, but I gotta wake up early
          and deal with my car.

                    MALLORY
          Fuck your car, this is the bee's
          knees.

                    ANGELA
               (looking at her phone)
          One review on Yelp. Says all
          proceeds go to Red Cross. That's
          cool.

                    HARPER
               (a little afraid)
          Bailey's right, you know, it's
          getting kinda late, and maybe --

                    NATHAN
          Harper, I _promised_ you a fun night.

Harper feigns a smile. Wants to tell him that she'd rather
leave. But doesn't.

EXT. HAUNTED HOUSE - NIGHT

Nathan puts his lucky BAT in Evan's trunk. The rest of the
group follows his lead, leaving behind the more cumbersome
parts of their COSTUMES, before making their way across the
parking lot.

In the faraway distance, they see another GROUP OF FRIENDS
disappear into the haunted house, laughing and having fun.

Our group is about half game, half ready for bed.

They're greeted by someone in a CLOWN **MASK**. The mask is
vintage: simple, clean, innocent. The kind of costume your
grandparents wore for Halloween.

*A quick NOTE about the MASKS: _All of the costumed characters
we encounter at this haunted house will wear VINTAGE
HALLOWEEN MASKS. We'll find out why later._*

                    NATHAN
          Uh, six tickets please?

The CLOWN doesn't respond. Just stares blankly ahead.

                    BAILEY
               (annoyed)
          Hello. We'd like to enter your rape-
          y establishment.

The CLOWN turns to Bailey. He holds up two enclosed FISTS,
miming for the group to choose one.

Bailey taps the LEFT FIST. The CLOWN opens his hand
revealing: NOTHING.

Evan taps the RIGHT FIST. The CLOWN opens his right hand
revealing: ALSO NOTHING.

The CLOWN reaches behind Bailey's head and pretends to pull a
KEY from her ear.

                    ANGELA
          All right. I'm giving this five
          stars on Yelp. Nothing scarier than
          mimes doing shitty magic.

Bailey takes the key. She is ushered to a LOCK BOX. She
inserts the key and opens the door...

                    NATHAN
          What is it?

Inside is a stack of LIABILITY WAIVERS. The group gathers
around Bailey.

                    BAILEY
          It's a release form. Says...
               (scanning)
          **HAUNTED HOUSE RULES. Rule number
          one:** Stay on the marked path at all
          times. **Rule number two:** Never touch
          the actors. **Number three:** You will
          be prompted to do certain actions.
          Please do exactly as you are told.
          This is for your safety.

Harper inhales. And her throat closes. She's not exhaling.
Not even a breath.

                    BAILEY
                 (reading)
          And lastly, **rule number four:** All
          cell phones must be surrendered to
          the lock box before entering. You
          may keep the lock box key until you
          return from the attraction.

Bailey holds up the release forms, suspicious. The group
mulls it over.

                    BAILEY
          Soooo basically, we sign our lives
          away.

                    MALLORY
          That's how you know it's good! This
          is like those "BLACKOUT" haunts
          they rave about on Reddit.

JUST THEN WE HEAR A SCREAM FROM DEEP INSIDE THE WAREHOUSE.

The group LAUGHS. Alright, this seems like fun.

Everyone starts signing the forms and surrendering their
PHONES in the lock box.

Mallory refreshes the CAST LIST one last time, then
begrudgingly parts with her phone.

                    EVAN
                 (scanning the form)
          Small print, small print... "Health
          insurance?" Fuck no...

Something catches Evan's eye. He looks up at the CLOWN.

                    EVAN
          You _really_ need my home address?

The CLOWN doesn't respond, staring Evan into submission.

                    EVAN
                 (under his breath)
          ...better not be sending penis
          enhancement ads to my dad. He's
          been through enough.

Harper signs the form. She starts to put her PHONE in the
lock box, but hesitates.

                    NATHAN
          Everything okay?

                    HARPER
          You know what, you guys go ahead.
          Think I'm just gonna call a ride.

                    EVAN
          You should take a Lyft.

Nathan looks a little hurt. Takes it personally.

                    NATHAN
          Out here, all by yourself?

                    HARPER
          Shouldn't take too long. Probably
          just a ten minute wait for a ride.

Harper loads her LYFT APPLICATION, starts typing in her MOM'S
ADDRESS but notices another TEXT from the anonymous number:

                    I SEE YOU

Harper looks up, terrified. Scans the parking lot. Then the
gravel pathway. Are those HEADLIGHTS in the distance?

Nathan notices something's wrong.

                    NATHAN
          We'll be done in ten minutes
          anyway, why don't you just come
          with and then I'll make sure Evan
          gets you home.

Harper nods. Safer to stay with friends than out here alone.

                    HARPER
          Okay, but you better stay close.

Nathan smiles. He takes Harper's hand and pulls her along.

               THEY ENTER THE HAUNTED HOUSE

INT. HAUNTED HOUSE, ENTRANCE HALL - NIGHT

Harper pauses, relieved.

The entrance is rather innocuous. A long hall with grey
walls, smooth and flat. The paint blotchy and unfinished,
clearly the work of volunteers. It's dark inside, but could
be darker. There are some rubber bats hanging from the
ceiling. And several plastic Jack-O-Lanterns along the floor
that could've been bought at Party City.

MUSIC plays through shitty speakers. Is it John Carpenter's
Halloween score? Is it the Tales from the Crypt theme? No.
Just some midi knock-off that's more annoying than scary.

It's all very benign and unthreatening. Pathetic, actually.

But our group is huddled close together anyway. They're
practically silent, moving slowly in anticipation of the
first scare - which could come from any direction.

The way they move, and how they react to their surroundings,
captures that universal feeling of going through a haunted
attraction with a group of friends - where everyone is
laughing and joking, and yeah it's kinda scary, but not
really life-threatening, which is what makes it fun, and
makes everyone *giggly* and *goofy* and *loud* - really, really
LOUD - because the louder you are the less scary it is when --

                    SKELETON
          BOO!

-- a SKELETON pops out of the wall to startle you. And yes,
it got the jump scare, but fuck. Really? A plastic skeleton?
It's not even a creepy one. It's actually kind of cute.

                    BAILEY
          This is supposed to be scary?

Nathan looks down to his arm, which HARPER IS NOW HUGGING.

                    EVAN
          The only thing that scares Bailey
          is being seen at the drive-thru
          window of McDonald's.

                    BAILEY
               (embarrassed)
          I don't go to McDonald's.

Bailey places her KITTY EARS on the skeleton's head.

                    EVAN
               (under his breath)
          ...more than twice a week.

INT. HAUNTED HOUSE, BLOOD HALL - NIGHT

The group turns a corner and enters a new corridor. Blood
spatter is painted on the walls and floor. The color is too
orange to be convincing as real.

Harper lets go of Nathan's arm. Feels okay about this, like she's gonna make it through without losing her shit.

They follow a STROBING LIGHT into a VORTEX TUNNEL.

INT. HAUNTED HOUSE, VORTEX TUNNEL - NIGHT

The vortex tunnel is made up of three aluminum rollers connected to a motor. The motor powers a large cylinder to spin around a bridge - causing extreme vertigo as people walk through.

What makes this tunnel particularly disorienting, is there are no customary handrails. And the further across the bridge our group gets, the faster the cylinder spins, causing most, if not all, of our group to buckle over to their hands and knees.

There's a low, plaintive MOAN coming from up ahead.

INT. HAUNTED HOUSE, DUNGEON - NIGHT

They stumble into a dungeon room, if you could even call it that. A square box no bigger than a small studio apartment.

The MOAN seems to come from a FIGURE across the way wearing a BLACK CLOAK.

Evan, still dizzy, approaches the figure and SMACK -- <u>hits his face on an invisible Plexiglas wall that bisects the room in half</u>.

The group laughs.

The figure turns at the sound. A WITCH **MASK** covers their face. They stand over a steaming cauldron, relentlessly stirring the pot with an IRON ROD.

We realize the MOAN isn't coming from the figure, it's coming from the BODY BAG on the floor.

The WITCH unzips the body bag. Inside is a YOUNG WOMAN, bound by ZIP TIES, half-conscious, starting to wake.

What happens next is a little shocking, if only because everything else in this place has been so pedestrian...

The WITCH pulls the IRON ROD out of the boiling cauldron. The rod glows a bright fiery orange.

The Young Woman begins to SCREAM. Writhing around on the ground, trying to break free of the zip ties.

Her performance is real and convincing. Not like the
community theater actors that usually work the local haunt...
this woman actually seems terrified.

                    YOUNG WOMAN
          HELP ME HELP ME HELP ME HELP ME

The WITCH pushes the red-hot IRON ROD down onto the woman and
her FACE INSTANTLY MELTS TO THE FLOOR LIKE CANDLE WAX.

The group watches in shock. Harper grabs Nathan's hand again.
Is this real?

The WITCH cackles, then suddenly SHOOOOOSH.... BLACK SMOKE
fills the Plexiglas cubicle. The smoke slowly dissipates and
we see the dungeon is now EMPTY.

                    BAILEY
                (disbelief)
          Holy shit, what?

                    EVAN
                (disbelief)
          Did you see how real that looked?
          They are not fucking around here.

A SMALL PASSAGEWAY opens in the wall.

                    NATHAN
          Onward.

INT. HAUNTED HOUSE, MAZE ENTRANCE - NIGHT

Nathan leads his friends into another corridor.

This one is completely unfinished. No decorations. Zero bells
and whistles. Just a spot of graffiti on the floor where
someone wrote in PURPLE SPRAY PAINT **"Hi"**. An odd choice to
say the least.

The group responds as they pass over the paint --

                    NATHAN
                (to the floor)
          Hello.

                    BAILEY
                (to the floor)
          Bonjour.

                    EVAN
                (to the floor)
          Aloha.

Their voices fall DEAD against the raw wood paneling.

They come to a FORK with two diverging paths. In the same spray paint, the word:

                    M A Z E
                    <---->

Bailey grabs Nathan and Angela, pulling them towards the LEFT PASSAGE <

                         BAILEY
              We'll go this way, you guys go that
              way!

Harper is pulled by Evan and Mallory to the RIGHT PASSAGE >

Harper and Nathan appeal. They wanted to stay together. But it's too late. <u>They are already inside the MAZE.</u>

                              INT. MAZE > SPIDER ROOM - NIGHT

Harper, Evan, and Mallory enter the RIGHT PASSAGE. Spider webs everywhere. Floor to ceiling. Masses of silk.

They peel through the room in disgust, which quickly turns to horror, as they realize there are REAL SPIDERS everywhere... not just the floor, the walls, the ceiling... but in their HAIR, their CLOTHES, their MOUTHS --

                         MALLORY
              Ew. What? WHAT?! IT'S IN MY FUCKING
              MOUTH --
                   (coughing, spitting)
              -- IN MY MOUTH!!!

                         EVAN
              Did you know that the Daddy Long
              Legs is actually the most deadly
              spider in the world, but their
              fangs are too short to --

                         MALLORY
              -- FUCK SPIDERS.

The back wall seems to dead end. THREE COFFINS stand upright, evenly spaced, flush against the wall.

Unsure how to proceed, Evan opens each coffin one by one. The process is suspenseful every time, but the search yields nothing. <u>All the coffins are empty.</u>

                        EVAN
              Where are we supposed to go?

Harper examines the coffins for herself. Sure enough, the
first one is empty. She opens the second coffin. Yep, that
one's empty too. She closes the coffin and WE HEAR A CREAKING
NOISE...

Harper stops.

                        HARPER
              What was that?

Harper opens the second coffin again. She feels the back
panel, notices the hinges drilled into the wood.

                        HARPER
              It's a door.

                        MALLORY
              But how do we open it?

                        HARPER
              Think it only opens when the coffin
              is closed.

                        EVAN
              Let's find out.

Evan steps in. Closes himself inside. He waits in DARKNESS
for a beat, and then...

The back wall of the coffin opens into a new room.

                        EVAN
                    (on the other side)
              It worked!

Harper looks at Mallory, unsure.

                        HARPER
              I'm not crazy about tight spaces.

                        MALLORY
              Then get it over with, "sweet
              cheeks"!

Harper opens the coffin and closes herself inside. She waits
in DARKNESS even longer than Evan, but eventually gets
through to the other side.

                        HARPER
                    (on the other side)
              I'm through, Mallory.

Finally, Mallory enters the coffin. Closes herself inside just like the others. But this time, the door never opens.

Mallory knocks on the door.

>   MALLORY
>   It's not working...

Now Mallory's starting to get scared. She knocks a little harder. Pushes the walls. What the fuck is going on!?

>   ...she's about to find out.

A hole in the top of the coffin slides open and THOUSANDS OF SPIDERS RAIN DOWN UPON MALLORY'S HEAD AS SHE SCREAMS AND THRASHES LIKE IT'S THE END OF THE WORLD.

INT. MAZE > SPIDER ROOM - OTHER SIDE OF COFFINS - NIGHT

The coffin door bursts opens, and Mallory comes rushing out, shaking and brushing all the tiny insects off her body, tears in her eyes, voice hoarse --

>   EVAN
>   -- Mallory! Mallory, calm down!

Hell no she doesn't want to calm down. This is the absolute worst thing that could ever happen to her --

>   EVAN
>   -- Mallory! Look!

Mallory takes a breath. Looks to the ground and realizes what Evan already knows... THE SPIDERS ARE RUBBER. IT'S NOT REAL.

>   MALLORY
>   (biggest sigh of relief)
>   Fuck spiders.

Evan grabs a RECEIPT off the ground.

>   EVAN
>   (reading)
>   Skeletons. Spiders. Masks.
>   (to Mallory/Harper)
>   It's a receipt from Party City.
>   Lazy bastards bought all this shit
>   a couple days ago.

>   MALLORY
>   No wonder it looks thrown together.
>   My middle school production of CATS
>   had better production design.

The Spider Room funnels to a vacant wall. There's a SQUARE HOLE near their feet. Appears to be some kind of CRAWL SPACE. <u>There are no other doors or ways ahead</u>.

> EVAN
> Who's first?

Harper gazes into the tunnel, which is PITCH BLACK.

> HARPER
> I'm not going in there.

INT. MAZE < LEFT PASSAGE - NIGHT

Nathan, Bailey and Angela enter the LEFT PASSAGE. The hall is dimly lit, with black walls only a shoulder-width apart.

Nathan's shoulder brushes the wall --

> BAILEY
> -- STOP RIGHT NOW.

Nathan freezes. Bailey swipes a finger across his shoulder. Holds it up... WET BLACK PAINT.

Nathan grabs his arm and realizes it's covered. The walls seem to glisten with FRESH PAINT.

> NATHAN
> Nothing like waiting 'til the last
> minute to paint the walls.

Bailey tries to wipe the paint off her finger, but can't.

> BAILEY
> (realizing)
> That's not paint... it's <u>oil</u>.

The passage winds around a series of turns which open to...

INT. MAZE < MIRROR ROOM - NIGHT

A MIRROR MAZE, where every wall is a reflective surface.

The only available light emits from cheap NEON FLOOR LIGHTS (the kind you'd see in theater aisles), which means it's hard to find an exit and easy to run into your own reflection.

Bailey braces her hands against the mirrors to guide her way through. Her reflection is multiplied to infinity.

38.

Bailey poses in front of a CURVED MIRROR. The warped
reflection makes her look super-model skinny.

                    BAILEY
                  (in awe)
            Every girl needs one of these in
            her dorm.

                    ANGELA
                  (notices something)
            That's weird...

Angela approaches from behind. Her eyes narrow.

                    ANGELA
            There's no gap between the
            reflection.

                    BAILEY
            So?

                    ANGELA
            It's a two-way mirror. My cousin
            Eric's a criminal psychiatrist.

The three look into the curved mirror, wondering who could be
on the other side, looking back.

                                    INT. MAZE > TUNNEL - NIGHT

Harper follows her friends through the tunnel, crawling on
her hands and knees. Darkness in every direction.

                    HARPER
            I'm not going in the tunnel.

                    EVAN
            We're already in the tunnel,
            Harper.

We hear a loud KNOCK.

                    EVAN
            Shit, dead end. We gotta turn
            around.

                    MALLORY
            Are you kidding me. It's too tight
            to turn around.

                    EVAN
            You're just drunk. Shuffle
            backwards and find a different way.

We don't really see them shuffle, so much as HEAR them. Arms
brushing the walls, feeling their way through, hoping to find
a new path in the dark.

                    MALLORY
          Gonna have so many splinters when I
          get home.

                    EVAN
          Found a path. Stay close.

There's a loud CRACK.

                    HARPER
                 (whispering)
          You hear that?

Everyone stops moving. Gets deadly silent. Listening.

THE WOOD FLOORS OF THE TUNNEL CREAK AND GROAN.

A SCRATCHING SOUND INTERRUPTS. ROUGH. FRANTIC. LIKE A DOG
PAWING AT SOMETHING.

                    EVAN
                 (whispering)
          Is that you guys?

                    HARPER
                 (whispering)
          Shhh.

SOUNDS OF MOVEMENT THROUGH THE TUNNEL.

COMING TOWARDS THEM.

GETTING CLOSER.

                    HARPER
                 (afraid)
          Keep moving, Evan.

A small light appears in the distance. Harper and Evan
clamber towards the opening as fast as they can.

They squeeze out of the exit of the tunnel and turn...

                    HARPER
          Where's Mallory?

Mallory is not with them.

INT. MAZE < LABORATORY - NIGHT

Nathan, Bailey, and Angela step into a rusty industrial room
fashioned like a Mad Scientist's lair.

GLASS BEAKERS line a counter, each filled with colored
liquids. The equipment looks like it could be used to cook
Meth.

In the center of the lab, a SKELETON is splayed upon an
AUTOPSY TABLE.

                    NATHAN
          There's some serious stank up in
          here.

Nathan approaches the skeleton and recoils.

                    ANGELA
          It's formaldehyde. Skeleton's
          covered in it.

                    BAILEY
          What's with the glory holes?

THREE HOLES have been cut into the wall, only large enough
for an arm to fit through. A message has been scrawled above:

GUESS THE BODY PARTS

Nathan stares into the first hole. It's completely dark. No
one wants to stick their hand inside.

                    ANGELA
          Pussies.

Angela shoves her hand into **HOLE #1**.

                    ANGELA
          OHMYGOD. GET IT OFF!

                    BAILEY
              (panic)
          What is it?!

Angela whips her hand from Hole #1 --

                    ANGELA
          BRAINS!

Angela laughs as she flicks SPAGHETTI (aka brains) from her
fingers. Bailey sighs with embarrassment. And relief.

They stare at **HOLE #2**. All wondering who will be next...

                    NATHAN
          Alright, I got this.

Nathan slowly reaches inside Hole #2.

                    NATHAN
          Hmmmm. Feels small.

He shoves his arm in further...

                    NATHAN
          Round.

FURTHER...

                    NATHAN
          Smooth.

                    ANGELA
          Anatomically speaking... I think
          you're fondling Evan's scrotum.

                    NATHAN
          Bingo --

Nathan pulls his arm out holding GRAPES (aka eyeballs). He
pops one in his mouth.

                    BAILEY
          Gross.

Nathan and Angela look toward Bailey. It's her turn.

                    BAILEY
          Fine.

Bailey takes a deep breath, pushes her sleeve up, and slowly
slides her hand inside **HOLE #3**.

                    BAILEY
          Should I be feeling anything yet?

Slides her arm in deeper.

                    BAILEY
          ...hmmmm...

HER ARM IS ALMOST FULLY ENGULFED BY THE HOLE.

                    BAILEY
          I give up.

Bailey pulls her hand out. That was anticlimactic. But wait...

Something's missing.

> BAILEY
> Fuck. My ring.

She stares into Hole #3. Can't see anything.

> NATHAN
> What ring?

> BAILEY
> Must've fallen off.

> ANGELA
> Sure you had it on?

> BAILEY
> Yes, I'm sure. Harper's gonna kill
> me. It's her mom's ring.

Bailey reaches back inside. Struggles for a moment.

> BAILEY
> Got it!

PLINK! Oh no, the ring slips. She frowns at the distinct sound of her ring falling out of reach.

Bailey's arm sinks deeper.

> BAILEY
> (distraught)
> ...we can't lose Harper's
> ring...it's important to her...

Nathan gets an idea and shoves his hand into Hole #2.

> NATHAN
> Maybe I can - wedge it, you know -
> from the other side.

Bailey & Nathan maneuver and struggle to pinch the ring between their hands, hidden somewhere behind the wall.

NATHAN SUDDENLY STOPS. His expression darkens.

> NATHAN
> You feel that?

> BAILEY
> Shut up.

                         NATHAN
              Something touched me. I'm serious.

Nathan cups his ear to the wall. The room goes quiet.

NATHAN EXPLODES INTO A HORRIFIC SCREAM!

BAILEY STARTS SCREAMING WHEN SHE REALIZES HOW SCARED HE IS!

ANGELA WATCHES IN HORROR, UNSURE WHAT TO DO, AND THEN --

Nathan starts LAUGHING. Just another bad joke.

-- BUT BAILEY DOESN'T RELENT. SHE SHRIEKS IN PAIN AS HER ARM
IS PULLED DEEPER INSIDE!

                         BAILEY
              IT HURTS IT HURTS IT HURTS!

Nathan tries to pull Bailey back from the hole, but SOMETHING
on the other side has taken hold.

                         NATHAN
                    (to Angela)
              Help!

Just then BAILEY FALLS BACK. Her arm is freed. And it looks
completely untouched.

Oh wait. Wait wait wait wait WAIT.

                         ANGELA
              Bailey...

Bailey rotates the underside of her arm --

BLOOD POOLS FROM A HUNDRED TINY LACERATIONS, razor-thin
slices that eat into her major veins.

                         BAILEY
              Ohmygod ohmygod ohmygod

Nathan backs away in shock.

Angela RIPS a foot of PLASTIC TUBING from the laboratory
display and TIES it around Bailey's arm as a TOURNIQUET.

THE PRESSURE CAUSES MORE BLOOD TO FLOW FROM BAILEY'S ARM.

                         BAILEY
              STOP STOP STOP!

                         ANGELA
              Nathan! Give me your shirt!

44.

                    NATHAN
     My jersey?

                    ANGELA
          Now!

Nathan pulls his jersey off over his undershirt. Angela
carefully wraps Bailey's arm to impede the blood flow and
THEN re-applies the make-shift tourniquet.

                    ANGELA
          My cousin Ken...
               (deep breath)
          ...is an E.M.T.

                         INT. MAZE > TUNNEL EXIT - NIGHT

Harper & Evan yell into the TUNNEL for their friend.

                    HARPER
          Mallory!

                    EVAN
          Mallory, can you hear us?! There's
          no spiders out here, I promise.

There's a SHUFFLING sound deep inside. HANDS and KNEES
scraping against plywood.

                    HARPER
          Follow our voices!

The SHUFFLING gets closer.

                    EVAN
          You're almost there!

A FIGURE crawls toward the TUNNEL EXIT. It's not Mallory...

Someone wearing a DEVIL MASK over a HOODED ROBE steps out
(maybe it's the same person Harper saw outside the bar).

Harper & Evan back away, confused and a little afraid.

                    EVAN
               (to the Devil)
          Our friend's still in there.

The DEVIL doesn't respond. Just stands coldly blocking the
tunnel.

Evan tries to maneuver around in order to keep searching for
Mallory, but the DEVIL won't move.

The DEVIL flips a switch. An EDISON BULB illuminates a YELLOW DOOR on the far wall.

Evan looks to Harper, unsure.

> HARPER
> Think he wants us to keep going.

Harper & Evan move toward the YELLOW DOOR.

The DEVIL follows closely behind. Never saying a word.

His very presence, the close proximity, his cold dominant demeanor, reminds Harper of Sam.

THE YELLOW DOOR STARTS TO RATTLE. IT'S AS IF SOMETHING OR SOMEONE IS TRYING TO GET OUT.

Brummmm... Harper and Evan listen.

Brummmmmmmm.... What is that?

BRRRRUUUUUMMMMMMMMMM!

> EVAN
> (realizing)
> Chainsaw.

THE ROAR OF THE CHAINSAW INTENSIFIES. THE DOOR BEGINS TO SHAKE VIOLENTLY.

They pass one of those EMERGENCY EXIT SIGNS that all modern Haunted Houses have, in case the attraction is too intense.

Harper thinks about running through the exit and ending this all right now. But she reminds herself, this is all just part of the show. Everything. Is. Going. To. Be. Just. Fine.

INT. SLIDE - NIGHT

They open the YELLOW DOOR slowly; nervous LEATHER FACE or some other fucked up member of the TEXAS CHAINSAW FAMILY will be on the other side, but...

NO ONE'S THERE. Just SPEAKERS in the ceiling emitting chainsaw noises.

> EVAN

Nice.

Below the speakers, a SLIDE descends into a dark passage. There is no other way to go.

SUDDENLY, THE SPEAKERS CUT OUT. SILENCE.

And then...

Somewhere below...

From the bottom of the dark passage...

The growl of a REAL CHAINSAW *Brum-BRUMMMMMMMMMMMMMMMM!!*

Harper notices the DEVIL behind them, watching.

> HARPER
> I'll go first.

Harper sits on top of the slide. Smiles like she's not scared, but obviously is. She pushes off with her trembling hands...

     down

          down

               down

                    down

INT. GRAVEYARD - NIGHT

Harper slows to a stop at the bottom of the slide. Sees someone in a **ZOMBIE MASK** holding a gas-powered CHAINSAW.

The ZOMBIE shuffles toward her. His feet kick up dust. The space behind him has been designed to resemble a GRAVEYARD.

Harper watches the ZOMBIE, nervous, unsure what to do.

> HARPER
> ...hi?

The ZOMBIE raises his CHAINSAW --

Harper flinches --

The ZOMBIE brings the saw down on her shoulder --

NOTHING HAPPENS.

Harper realizes the chain has been removed from the saw (a common gimmick in most haunted houses).

Evan surfaces at the bottom. The ZOMBIE does the same routine to him. Evan flinches too.

> EVAN
> Dude, outta my safe-space.

Evan shoves the ZOMBIE. The ZOMBIE staggers back, caught off guard. He stares at Evan, silent.

Regret wrinkles onto Evan's face as he realizes "Oh shit I just broke the rules."

The ZOMBIE nudges them forward into the graveyard; a square mud patch with four or five FAKE HEADSTONES scattered about.

Harper notices the ZOMBIE isn't following them into the graves. They get about halfway through and **REALIZE WHY...**

THE GRAVEYARD IS LIKE QUICK SAND.

HARPER'S FEET BEGIN TO SINK INTO THE GROUND.

> HARPER
> Evan...

SHE TRIES TO GRAB A NEARBY HEADSTONE.

BUT THE MORE SHE MOVES, THE DEEPER SHE DROWNS.

UNTIL HER ENTIRE BODY IS SUBMERGED.

AND WE CAN ONLY SEE HER FACE.

SCREAMING FOR HELP.

> HARPER
> EVAN!!

The ZOMBIE backs away into the shadows.

Evan's starting to sink too. He spots an INDUSTRIAL HOSE, running water into the dirt. He holds the hose and grabs Harper's hand just as it disappears below.

> EVAN
> HARPER, HOLD ON!

Evan pulls Harper up, using everything he's got.

The dirt composite expands and contracts, until finally...

Harper's arm materializes...

And then her shoulder...

Her face...

Body...

Together they struggle to the surface. Evan drags Harper to solid ground.

> EVAN
> Harper?!

> HARPER
> (gathers her breath)
> I'm okay I'm okay.

They wring mud and grime off their clothes, laughing nervously. A little shaken. Can't decide if that was fun or dangerous or both.

There's a RED DOOR up ahead.

INT. RED DOOR ROOM - NIGHT

Harper & Evan enter the RED DOOR and see --

NATHAN, BAILEY, & ANGELA HUDDLED TOGETHER ON THE OTHER SIDE OF THE ROOM. BAILEY IS CRYING. NATHAN AND ANGELA LOOK SCARED.

> NATHAN
> Don't close that --

THE RED DOOR SLAMS SHUT AND LOCKS BEHIND THEM.

> NATHAN
> (defeated)
> -- door.

> ANGELA
> Shit!

> HARPER
> What's going on?!

Harper & Evan rush over to their friends.

> NATHAN
> We have to get out of here, we have
> to um we have to uh we have to uh,
> we, we, we...

Harper has never seen Nathan this frightened.

Evan notices Bailey's arm.

                    EVAN
          Bailey, fuck are you okay?

Bailey's in a daze, barely registers Evan's question.

                    BAILEY
          ...doesn't hurt... anymore...

                    NATHAN
          Where's where's where's Mallory?

                    EVAN
          She was with us in the --

                    HARPER
          -- are we trapped?

Harper has just noticed the CHAIN LINK FENCE that cuts the
room in half, trapping them inside, like a CAGE. The other
side of the fence is obscured by a BLACK CURTAIN.

                    BAILEY
          We're not trapped, we're just
          supposed to wait here, and then we
          can go... we can go if we wait
          here...

                    HARPER
          Wait here for what?

THE BLACK CURTAIN OPENS.

Behind the fence we see the WITCH dragging a BODY BAG into
view.

Nathan runs at the fence.

                    NATHAN
          Hey! Someone's hurt in here! We
          need help!

The WITCH unzips the body bag and we see MALLORY inside.
She's unconscious.

                    EVAN
          Hey, what the fuck! Hey!

The guys hit the fence, trying to break through.

                    BAILEY
               (delirious)
          ...it's just part of the show, if
          we wait here, then we can go....

Bailey has lost a lot of blood. Her face is pale. She's terrified, but trying to hide it.

> NATHAN
> Mallory, wake up!

> EVAN
> Mallory, what's going on?! What are you doing?!

> ANGELA
> Maybe she's just acting?

The WITCH moves to her CAULDRON. She pulls out a HOT IRON ROD from the brew --

> NATHAN
> HEY, NO!

-- AND STABS IT INTO MALLORY'S FACE AS THE BLACK CURTAIN CLOSES.

> EVAN
> HEY! HEY!

TIME SLOWS DOWN. LIVE SOUND IS CONSUMED BY AN OMINOUS DRONE.

THE GROUP STARES IN STUNNED SILENCE. THEY HAVE NO IDEA WHAT TO DO OR SAY. THEY JUST LET THE AWFULNESS SINK IN. AS THEY REALIZE... *OH MY FUCKING GOD THIS IS REAL*.

PANIC SETS IN. THE GROUP REACTS. THRASHING AND CRYING. SILENT SCREAMS. CONFUSION AND DESPERATION.

A BLUE DOOR OPENS on the other side of the room. It's the only way out.

> NATHAN
> No! Fuck that! We're not going through that door.

> ANGELA
> Oh my god what's happening.

> BAILEY
> (crying)
> I wanna go home.

> ANGELA
> (no voice)
> What's happening, what's happening.

Nathan moves over to Bailey, tries to keep her conscious as she continues losing blood.

Harper sits in the corner of the room, her head collapses into her hands, starts to hyperventilate.

>   NATHAN
>   HELP! WE NEED HELP! PLEASE!
>   SOMEBODY HELP US!

Nathan's voice grows hoarse. He realizes his efforts are futile. Tries to compose his thoughts.

>   NATHAN
>   Does, does anyone have a phone?

>   ANGELA
>   (disbelief)
>   They're all in the fucking lock
>   box.

>   NATHAN
>   That's okay, we just need to get to
>   the lock box and... and call 911. Who
>   has the key?

>   EVAN
>   I don't have it.

>   NATHAN
>   Anyone?

Everyone frantically searching their pockets.

>   NATHAN
>   Please don't tell me Mallory had
>   it.

>   BAILEY
>   ...here...

Bailey holds up the KEY. Nathan takes it.

>   NATHAN
>   Thank you, Bailey, thank you.

>   EVAN
>   (scared)
>   Now what, man? We go back the way
>   we came?

>   HARPER
>   I saw an exit.

Everyone turns to Harper, whose head is still in her hands.

                    NATHAN
          Where?

Harper looks at the RED DOOR.

                    HARPER
          Back that way.

                    NATHAN
          An exit? Like an exit outside?

                    HARPER
          Emergency exit.

Nathan moves to the RED DOOR. Tries the handle. It's locked,
of course, but loose. He runs his shoulder into it a few
times. Doesn't really give.

                    NATHAN
          Can we break this? Evan?

                    EVAN
          So... so... maybe if I... Angela do
          you have any hairpins left?

Angela removes her NURSE HAT. Hands Evan her last three
HAIRPINS.

                    EVAN
          Let me, uh... I can...

Evan nervously approaches the RED DOOR. Fashions two of the
hairpins into a LOCK PICK KIT. Goes to work on the handle.

                    EVAN
          Shit.

                    NATHAN
          What's wrong?

                    EVAN
          Nothing, nothing.

Evan is struggling. Clearly something's wrong.

                    NATHAN
          Can I help?

                    EVAN
          I got it, I got it --

SNAP! One of the HAIRPINS breaks.

                    EVAN
          Fuck, sorry!

Evan inserts the final hairpin into the lock, tries again.
Doesn't seem to be making any progress.

                    EVAN
               (struggling)
          It's a... it's a two-way lock... a
          Kwikset two-way... I don't think I
          can...

                    ANGELA
          What happened to "I can lock pick
          anything"?

                    EVAN
          Yeah, I meant like "anything", like
          "a locker". I'm the equipment
          manager, not Robert De Niro from
          "HEAT".

                    NATHAN
          Evan, we need you to get through
          that door.

                    EVAN
          It's fine, I can do it... I just
          need... so...
               (beat)
          Maybe if we go a little bit
          further...

                    NATHAN
          No.

                    EVAN
          ...not all of us. Just you and me.
          We go a little bit further, we find
          something, like a crowbar, to
          breach the hinges.

                    NATHAN
          ...that's where they want us to go.
          They will be waiting for us...

                    EVAN
          ...I know. I know. I'm not saying
          let's keep going. I'm saying... I'm
          saying: We go a little bit further,
          and find something. Anything.
          Right? To break this door down.

                    NATHAN
                 (pacing wildly)
        Fuck. Okayokayokayokay. Right.
        Yeah, okay. I'll go, just, a quick
        look. I can do it. Um. Just keep
        working on the handle.

Nathan moves to the BLUE DOOR. Pauses. Starts to hand over
the LOCK BOX KEY to Evan.

                    NATHAN
        In case anything happens.

Evan refuses the key.

                    EVAN
        Nothing's gonna happen. Just come
        right back.

Nathan nods.

INT. BLACK CORRIDOR - NIGHT

Nathan passes through the BLUE DOOR into a darkened hallway –
either too long or too dark to tell where it ends.

And as much as Nathan would like to hurry, he's not going to
run blindly into a trap.

He takes a few steps.

A HIGH-PITCH HISS startles Nathan to a stop as WHITE FOG
emits from tubes running along the floorboards. The fog
obscures a SLIM PASSAGE ahead.

INT. SUFFOCATION TUNNEL - NIGHT

The slim passage is what's known in the Haunted Housing
industry as a "Suffocation Tunnel" or "Claustrophobia
Tunnel".

It's essentially a tight hallway, with large INFLATED FABRIC
PANELS on each wall, that press together from both sides,
creating the simulated feeling of being suffocated as people
pass through.

Nathan squeezes into the black fabric and instantly realizes
how it got its name: it's hard to breathe inside, and nearly
impossible to see anything further than a couple inches in
either direction.

He tries to hurry through, but it gets harder and harder to move the deeper he goes, until --

A MOTOR WHIRS to life, and suddenly the panels begin to fill with air, dangerously locking Nathan in place.

                                        BACK TO:

INT. RED DOOR ROOM - NIGHT

Harper and Angela sit on either side of Bailey, doing their best to comfort her.

                    ANGELA
                 (in shock)
            They have everything. Our
            addresses. The names of our
            parents...

Angela notices something.

                    ANGELA
                 (terrified)
            Evan. What are you doing?

Evan is on his stomach, peering under the BLACK CURTAIN that covers the chain link fence.

He looks past the fence where Mallory's body used to be.

                    EVAN
            She's gone. There must be a trick
            door on the other side somewhere.

                    ANGELA
                 (terrified)
            Just leave it. We don't want to
            piss them off.

                    EVAN
            One sec.

                    ANGELA
                 (terrified)
            Evan, don't.

                    EVAN
            Come here.

Angela begrudgingly crawls over to Evan.

>   EVAN
>   Is your arm small enough to fit
>   through the fence?

>   ANGELA
>   What?

>   EVAN
>   There's a metal poker thing right
>   there, but I can't reach it.

Angela looks under the curtain. It's dark, but she sees the
IRON ROD that Evan's talking about, only a couple feet away.

>   ANGELA
>   So?

>   EVAN
>   So we can use it to break the door
>   hinges.

Angela contorts her fingers into a spear-like shape and
pushes her tiny arm through one of the chain links. It's
rusty and an extremely tight fit. She has to move slow.

>   ANGELA
>   I feel like my cousin Amy. She's a
>   proctologist.

>   EVAN
>   How many fucking cousins do you
>   have?

>   ANGELA
>   Forty-six.

INT. SUFFOCATION TUNNEL - NIGHT

Nathan is still trapped in the tunnel. The walls continue to
INFLATE. His face is purple. Blood is pushing into his eyes.

His hand presses against his pocket, pushing inside, fishing
for something, trying to get a hold of THE LOCK BOX KEY.

Nathan forces the key out of his pocket. He angles the sharp
tip into the inflating wall.

Just as he's about to take his final breath --

PSSSSSHHHHHHHHHHHHHHH! The key punctures the surface and all
the air deflates out of the wall panels.

Nathan topples.

The lock box key drops to the floor...

And the floor is comprised of metal grates...

Which is why the key starts to fall through the cracks, teetering on the edge back and forth.

                    NATHAN
          ...shit, shit...

Nathan's hand slams down to catch the key, but the momentum pushes it through.

                    NATHAN
          ...no.

Nathan takes a beat. He has lost the lock box key somewhere down below.

He stands, afraid of what's ahead. But he has to keep going.

                    NATHAN
               (escaping his lips)
          ...lean into the pitch, lean into
          the pitch...

Fog creeps around a corner. He follows it around the bend. Stops dead.

                    NATHAN
          Shit...

Nathan's eyes glaze with fear.

THE SILHOUETTES OF A DOZEN BODIES LEAN AGAINST BOTH SIDES OF A LONG FOG-FILLED CORRIDOR. It's difficult to tell if these are mannequins, or statues, or...

ONE OF THE BODIES MOVES.

Nathan flinches. Did he imagine that?

WHACK!

A faint NOISE in the distance, like shutters in the wind.

Nathan gathers all his courage.

                                        BACK TO:

INT. RED DOOR ROOM - NIGHT

As Angela and Evan struggle for the rod, Harper turns to
Bailey who is terrified.

                    BAILEY
          What if it's Sam...

                    HARPER
     What?

                    BAILEY
          Who's doing this... he's crazy, he
          could've followed us here...

Harper holds back tears. Lies to her friend.

                    HARPER
          No, he wouldn't.

Angela's hand gets close to the iron, but it's just barely
out of reach. She pulls her arm out. Stretches. Tries again.

                    BAILEY
          How come we're not friends
          anymore...

                    HARPER
          What do you mean?

Harper knows it's true. And here they are, all that wasted
time, her friend hurting.

                    HARPER
          I don't know. So many things
          changed last year. I got an after
          school job. Orchestra practice on
          weekends...

                    BAILEY
          ...tell me a story?

                    HARPER
          A story? Okay, um. A story...
               (thinking)
          Remember freshman year, every time
          we got homesick, we'd read Harry
          Potter to each other? Think I know
          Sorcerer's Stone by heart, um...

                    BAILEY
          ...tell me a story about why you're
          sad.

Beat.

> HARPER
> Do you think I'm sad?

FLASH CUT: Young Harper plays with a doll in her bedroom.
She's startled by a LOUD NOISE.

> BAILEY
> ...I could always tell. I should've
> said something sooner...

Bailey closes her eyes in pain.

> BAILEY
> ...I'm sorry.

FLASH CUT: Young Harper hides under the bed.

Harper thinks a moment. Chooses her words carefully. Speaks
with emotional eyes.

> HARPER
> I grew up in a haunted house.

INT. BLACK CORRIDOR - NIGHT

Nathan approaches the first BODY of dozens. It is draped in
WHITE CLOTH like a ghost. The body stands threateningly
still. Impossible to tell if someone or something is
underneath.

He looks to his right, to another BODY, also covered in
white cloth. Neither appear to move, so Nathan continues.

WHACK. The noise Nathan heard earlier is LOUDER. Still can't
tell where it's coming from.

> NATHAN
> Someone there?

> > > BACK TO:

INT. RED DOOR ROOM - NIGHT

Bailey starts to breathe slower.

> BAILEY
> ...what kind of haunted house...
> was it like this one?

FLASH CUT: Harper's childhood home. Midwest suburbia. White picket fence. American Flag on the porch. SHOUTING INSIDE --

> HARPER
> No, it was different. I loved my
> house and hated it at the same
> time. It was where my dad would
> read to me. Where he taught me how
> to ride a bike. And where he hurt
> my mom.

*FLASH CUT: Harper's **FATHER** hits Harper's **MOTHER**. A RING flies off her finger and tumbles under the bed --*

> HARPER
> Whenever my dad would drink, I'd go
> to my room and hide under the bed.
> And one day, while I was hiding, he
> threw my mom across the floor. Like
> it was nothing. Like this is how
> things were supposed to be.

FLASH CUT: YOUNG HARPER hiding under the bed, her face red from crying. She reaches for the RING --

> HARPER
> I haven't been home in four years.
> But I keep having this recurring
> dream, where one day I go back,
> knock on the door, terrified my dad
> will answer and... my mom steps
> out. She tells me he's gone
> forever. She tells me: the house
> isn't haunted anymore.

Bailey looks to Harper, unable to speak. Tears forming in the corners of her eyes.

> BAILEY
> But the story has a happy ending...
> (beat)
> ...you got out.

Harper tries to smile, but knows deep down, in many ways she never got out. Her eyes drift from Bailey over to Angela.

> BAILEY
> I'm really sorry, Harper...

> HARPER
> For what?

> BAILEY
> ...I lost your mom's ring.

Angela's fingertips graze the end of the IRON ROD --

                    ANGELA
          OUCH!

-- and instantly recoil. She clutches her hand.

                    ANGELA
               (to Evan)
          Hot.

                    EVAN
          The other end.

The other end of the rod is even further out of reach. Angela
sticks her hand back through the rusty chain link.

                    ANGELA
          This is how you get tetanus.

INT. BLACK CORRIDOR - NIGHT

Nathan passes two more bodies. (And at this point, we're just
waiting for them to come alive.)

WHACK. An OPEN DOOR swings on its hinges.

                    NATHAN
          I need your help. We have money, we
          can pay whatever you want.

WHACK! The door slams closed against the frame. Nathan
hesitates to step any further before --

SWOOSH. The door springs open again. Something moves inside.

Nathan staggers back.

                    NATHAN
          Please.

He bumps into a body.

THE BODY MOVES.

Nathan turns.

THE BODY IS WEARING A **GHOST MASK.**

IT DISAPPEARS INTO THE FOG. IMPOSSIBLE TO PICK IT OUT AMONGST
THE MASS OF BODIES ALL AROUND.

                    NATHAN
                   (afraid)
           Please something really bad
           happened. My friend's hurt.

The GHOST steps out of the fog.

Gazes at Nathan for a long beat.

Then moves over to the wall and flips a switch:

BRIGHT OVERHEAD LIGHTS COME ON.

Nathan can now clearly see the man in the GHOST mask. He
wears a cheap bedsheet over his body. A dirty pair of NEW
BALANCE sneakers poke out from the frayed ends of his blue
jeans.

                    GHOST
           You saying you need help?

The VOICE behind the mask is so utterly normal and human that
Nathan nearly cries.

                    NATHAN
           Thank you thank you so much my
           name's Nathan I have no idea what's
           going on can you help us?

Long silence.

                    GHOST
           Yeah. Follow me.

The GHOST starts moving to the far door. The wrong way. The
way that leads deeper inside the haunted house.

                    NATHAN
           Okay. But the thing about that. Is.
           I told my friends I'd come right
           back. And... so, do you think you
           could come with me? Talk to
           everyone with me and we'll all go
           together?

                    GHOST
           Yeah.

Another long pause from the man in the mask.

                    GHOST
           Why don't you send everyone
           through. I'll go get help and meet
           you guys outside.

Nathan shakes his head, unsure.

>   NATHAN
>   Right. Right. Would you, I think it
>   would help - listen, we have a lot
>   of really scared people back there.
>   And it might give them some
>   comfort, if, someone who worked
>   here came back with me...

>   GHOST
>   Yeah.

Nathan doesn't like this. Another long pause.

>   GHOST
>   It's just... if it's urgent I
>   should get help.

Nathan's eyes, pleading.

>   GHOST
>   But I understand what you're
>   saying. Let me get something, I'll
>   be right back.

>   NATHAN
>   Okay, thank- thank you.

Nathan thinks he sees the GHOST grab something SHINY, but
maybe he's just imagining things.

>   BACK TO:

INT. RED DOOR ROOM - NIGHT

Angela's hand is gripped around the far end of the IRON ROD,
pulling it <u>CLOSER</u>

>   CLOSER

>   CLOSER

>   CLOSER

>   CLOSER

A BLACK BOOT COMES DOWN HARD ON ANGELA'S HAND.

BREAKING IT INSTANTLY.

ANGELA SCREAMS.

SHE DROPS THE IRON.

SOMEONE IS INSIDE THE FENCE.

WE SEE THE WITCH (WHO HAS BEEN HERE ALL ALONG) EXIT THROUGH A
TRICK DOOR IN THE WALL.

Evan pulls the iron rod the rest of the way through. He runs
immediately to the RED DOOR and starts whacking the HINGES.

                    GHOST (O.S.)
            What's going on!?

Everyone turns to find Nathan with the GHOST.

The GHOST looks at Bailey and Angela who are both in pain.
Sees how terrified everyone is...

                    GHOST
                (to Bailey)
            Jesus Christ. We need to get her
            out.

                    EVAN
            The fuck do you think I'm doing?

Evan keeps hitting the door.

                    GHOST
            No no no, don't do that -

                    EVAN
            There's an emergency exit on the
            other side.

                    GHOST
            But don't break the door -

                    EVAN
            I'll burn this place to the ground
            if I have to!

                    GHOST
            I have a key.

Evan immediately stops.

                    EVAN
            Where is it?

The GHOST ignores Evan and kneels to Angela. Sees her BLACK
BRUISED hand. Shakes his head.

GHOST
This isn't supposed to happen.

NATHAN
We just need to get out okay I
don't want to talk to your manager
or anything like that we didn't see
anything or do anything.

Angela looks directly at the GHOST.

ANGELA
(through tears)
We just want to leave.

The GHOST digs beneath his costume and grabs a ring of KEYS
attached to his belt.

INT. GRAVEYARD - NIGHT

The group backtracks. Harper & Nathan help Bailey along.

HARPER
The exit was this way.

Evan ushers everyone around the graveyard, avoiding the quick
sand.

EVAN
Watch out, careful.

They each climb the slide single file.

INT. MAZE > TUNNEL EXIT - NIGHT

Harper leads them to the EMERGENCY EXIT DOOR she saw earlier.

HARPER
Over here.

Evan pushes the handle. Doesn't budge.

He pushes again harder. Still won't open.

EVAN
Fucking knew it!

ANGELA
Read the door you idiot.

The door says:

PULL TO OPEN

Evan smiles, happy to be wrong for once.

EVAN PULLS THE DOOR OPEN.

A SOFT EMERGENCY BEEP GOES OFF.

LITTLE LIGHTS ON THE CEILING STROBE.

THE DOOR SWINGS WIDE OPEN.

THEY SEE...

...

...

...

NOTHING.

THERE IS NOTHING BEHIND THIS DOOR.

NOTHING OTHER THAN A CEMENT WALL.

> GHOST
> That makes sense, I didn't remember
> there being an exit here.

Harper looks at the TUNNEL. She considers it a moment.

> HARPER
> What if we crawl back through the
> maze?

> NATHAN
> (nodding)
> And keep going until we're at the
> entrance.

> GHOST
> If you want. But you can only go
> one at a time. There's a trap door
> in the tunnel that gets triggered
> if too many people are inside.

> NATHAN
> Trap door?

> GHOST
> We use it to capture people so we
> can put them in the show.
> (explaining)
> (MORE)

                    GHOST (cont'd)
          There's this whole thing with a
          witch where --

                    EVAN
          -- we know the fucking show, our
          friend is dead because of the show!

                    GHOST
          She's not dead. She's waiting
          outside for you guys. Probably
          wondering what's going on.
               (beat)
          Look, we're a little extreme here,
          but safety's a huge priority.

                    EVAN
          Safety? We've got two people who
          need to go to the hospital. MRIs, X-
          rays, ambulances. You're paying all
          the expenses. And then? We're gonna
          blow up our social media presence
          on your ass. Your whole
          establishment is going into the
          fucking ground. WHAT'S YOUR NAME?

                    GHOST
          ...

                    EVAN
          WHAT'S YOUR FUCKING NAME?

Harper holds Evan back, calming him down.

                    HARPER
               (softly)
          Sir, my name is Harper. Thank you
          for your help. Can you please tell
          us who you are?

                    GHOST
          You can call me Mitch.

                    HARPER
          Thank you, Mitch.

                    NATHAN
          And what's your full name?

                    GHOST
          You can call me Mitch.

Nathan takes the IRON ROD from Evan. The gesture could be
seen as a threat.

                    NATHAN
          I think we'd all feel more
          comfortable if you just took off
          your mask and told us your actual
          name.

                    GHOST
          I don't care which way you go, but
          you're almost at the end of the
          haunted house. It's probably
          farther if you go backwards.

                    EVAN
          We don't wanna go that way! You're
          not listening!

                    HARPER
              (to her friends)
          Why don't we, one at a time, head
          back through the tunnel.

                    EVAN
          Is that smart? Remember how dark it
          is in there?

                    HARPER
          I just want to get out of here.

                    NATHAN
              (to the GHOST)
          Mitch, do you have a flashlight?

                    GHOST
          I can get one.

                    NATHAN
          Where is it?

Nathan already knows the answer before he asks.

                    GHOST
          Back that way.

Evan shakes his head, defeated.

                    EVAN
          Okay, fuck, here's what I think:
              (deep breath)
          I vaguely remember my way around
          the tunnel. Give me the lock box
          key, I'll crawl through first, book
          it to the entrance, grab our phones
          and call for help.

                    NATHAN
          Okay. Mitch, do you have a copy of
          the lock box key?

                    EVAN
               (to Nathan)
          Don't you have it?

                    GHOST
          You're gonna have to talk to the
          clown about a replacement. You're
          supposed to hold onto that. It's
          policy.

                    EVAN
               (to Nathan)
          Dude I don't understand, you just
          had the key.

Nathan shakes his head, feels like he let everyone down.

                    NATHAN
          I'm sorry, guys.

                    EVAN
          What the hell, this is exactly why
          you're riding the bench. When it
          matters most and the pressure's on,
          you fall apart.

                    ANGELA
          Guys, this isn't the time, let's
          just get out of here. Evan?

                    EVAN
          Fuck policy. Fuck the Clown. Fuck
          the key. I can pick the lock box.
          So I'm first. We send Bitch through
          second. He can chill on the other
          side and wait for the rest of you.
          Nathan goes in third, with the
          "sharp instrument", in case Mitch
          needs a reminder that he's with us.

                    NATHAN
          Right, right.

                    EVAN
          Next goes Bailey and Angela, since
          they need the most help. Last goes
          Harper.

Harper swallows.

                         NATHAN
                      (to Harper)
                  You okay with that, Harper?

                         HARPER
                  Sounds fair.

Nathan nods.

                         HARPER
                  One thing though...
                      (turns to GHOST)
                  <u>I want your keys.</u>

INT. TUNNEL - NIGHT

Evan crawls through the dark tunnel.

INT. MAZE > TUNNEL EXIT - NIGHT

The group waits for Evan to give the "signal" that he's
through.

BEHIND THEM...

THEY HEAR A NOISE COMING FROM BELOW THE SLIDE.

Everyone sits up, alert.

Harper carries the KEY-RING to the YELLOW DOOR.

                         HARPER
                  Which one?

                         GHOST
                  Yellow, obviously.

Harper finds the YELLOW KEY and locks the door (making sure
no one can creep up on them from behind).

Then she puts her ear to it, listening for any sounds of
movement.

INT. TUNNEL - NIGHT

Evan sees light up ahead.

INT. MAZE > SPIDER ROOM - NIGHT

Evan squeezes out of the tunnel. He SLAPS the wall three
times and yells:

> EVAN
> I'm through!

INT. MAZE > TUNNEL EXIT - NIGHT

Nathan stands with the ROD aimed at the GHOST.

> NATHAN
> You're up.

The GHOST crawls into the tunnel.

INT. MAZE - NIGHT

Evan runs through the maze.

Everything looks different on the way back.

Completely different.

Did he miss a turn?

INT. TUNNEL - NIGHT

The GHOST sees light up ahead.

INT. MAZE > SPIDER ROOM - NIGHT

The GHOST slinks out of the tunnel. Stands. Looks around the
room. Spiderwebs matted down from where Evan ran through.

INT. MAZE > TUNNEL EXIT - NIGHT

Nathan paces nervously.

> NATHAN
> What's taking so long.

INT. MAZE > SPIDER ROOM - NIGHT

The GHOST stares at the far wall.

He taps it with his knuckle. Hears a hollow knock. Opens a
hidden COMPARTMENT and removes a TOOL KIT and some PLYWOOD.

He carries the TOOL KIT and PLYWOOD to the tunnel entrance.
POUNDS the wall three times and yells:

                         GHOST
          I'm in!

INT. MAZE > TUNNEL EXIT - NIGHT

                         NATHAN
          Finally.

Nathan enters the TUNNEL with the IRON ROD.

Harper is still listening at the YELLOW DOOR. She hears
FOOTSTEPS approaching.

INT. MAZE - NIGHT

Evan races around the maze in circles, completely LOST. Every
direction looks the same.

INT. TUNNEL - NIGHT

Nathan struggles through the tunnel. Hard to move, hard to
breathe. Hits his head on a dead end. Crawls back and tries a
different path.

All the while, there's an ominous THUMPING NOISE growing
closer.

It sounds like...

INT. MAZE > SPIDER ROOM - NIGHT

...NAILS BEING HAMMERED INTO A WALL.

We see the GHOST has placed the PLYWOOD over the tunnel hole,
hammering it into place, trapping Nathan inside.

INT. MAZE < MIRROR ROOM - NIGHT

Evan passes the TWO WAY MIRROR from earlier, but this time we
see the other side:

SOMEONE IN A **VAMPIRE MASK** WATCHES EVAN.

INT. MAZE > TUNNEL EXIT - NIGHT

The FOOTSTEPS stop right outside the YELLOW DOOR.

Harper holds her breath. Gets as quiet as she possibly can.

THE DOOR KNOB TURNS.

> HARPER
>
> No...

INT. TUNNEL - NIGHT

Nathan hits another dead end inside the tunnel. Pounds the wall out of frustration.

INT. MAZE > SPIDER ROOM - NIGHT

The GHOST watches the PLYWOOD flex as Nathan hits it from the other side.

The GHOST turns to pursue Evan.

INT. MAZE - NIGHT

Evan stumbles around a corner and --

> SKELETON
>
> **BOO!**

-- the SKELETON from earlier pops out. This time it scares the shit out of him. He flies back into the wall.

Evan takes a moment to collect himself. Recognizes Bailey's KITTY EARS atop the skeleton's head.

He's getting close.

INT. MAZE > TUNNEL EXIT - NIGHT

Harper hears the YELLOW DOOR unlock from the other side.

She grabs the handle.

> HARPER
> (screams to Bailey &
> Angela)
> RUN!

Bailey & Angela go white. They look into the tunnel.

                    BAILEY
          ...we have to wait for the
          signal...

                    ANGELA
               (into tunnel)
          Nathan! Hurry!

The YELLOW DOOR starts to push open. Harper leans against it, using all her weight to hold it closed.

                    HARPER
               (screaming)
          RUN! RUN! RUN!

Angela helps Bailey into the tunnel. She crawls in after.

THE YELLOW DOOR BURSTS OPEN.

HARPER IS THROWN TO THE GROUND.

THE DEVIL ENTERS HOLDING A PITCHFORK.

HE GOES TO THE TUNNEL.

REACHES INSIDE AND GRABS A LEG.

ANGELA IS YANKED OUT OF THE HOLE.

SHE'S TOO SCARED TO FIGHT BACK.

BEFORE HARPER CAN EVEN STAND TO HELP...

THE DEVIL DRIVES HIS PITCHFORK RIGHT INTO ANGELA'S FACE KILLING HER INSTANTLY.

Harper staggers to her feet.

The DEVIL holds gaze with her.

His eyes like two black marbles, soulless, piercing through the mask.

Harper runs through the YELLOW DOOR. She dives onto the slide...
          down
                    down
                              down
                                        down

INT. GRAVEYARD - NIGHT

The DEVIL right behind her, gaining so quickly, she's barely out of the slide before he lunges --

Harper turns, SCREAMS. The DEVIL shifts off balance, carelessly stepping into QUICK SAND.

He starts to sink, uses his PITCH FORK to stay afloat.

Harper runs through the RED DOOR --

INT. RED DOOR ROOM - NIGHT

-- throws it shut. Takes out the KEY-RING. Drops the keys. Picks them up. Rifles through them. Finds the RED KEY.

LOCKS THE DOOR.

INT. TUNNEL - NIGHT

Bailey pulls herself through complete darkness.

A voice up ahead...

                    NATHAN (O.S.)
          Who's there?

                    BAILEY
          Nathan?

                    NATHAN (O.S.)
          I'm at a dead end. We have to go
          back.

                    BAILEY
          Which way?

SHINK! A LOUD MECHANICAL SOUND followed by silence.

                    BAILEY
          Nathan?

Nothing.

                    BAILEY
          Nathan are you there?

INT. UNDERGROUND, TRAP DOOR - NIGHT

Nathan lies unconscious on concrete floor. He has fallen ten feet through a TRAP DOOR. His body spasms from the fall.

INT. RED DOOR ROOM - NIGHT

The RED DOOR starts to unlock from the other side.

Harper puts her key back in and re-locks the handle.

THE HANDLE UNLOCKS AGAIN.

SHE RE-LOCKS IT AGAIN.

UNLOCKS AGAIN.

RE-LOCKS.

Harper holds the key in place, trying to prevent the DEVIL on the other side from turning the lock, but the NICKEL PLATING IS STARTING TO WARP...

EXT. HAUNTED HOUSE - NIGHT

Evan runs out of the HAUNTED HOUSE.

All of the cars are gone. The barbed wire PERIMETER FENCE that surrounds the lot is now CLOSED.

Evan fishes the makeshift LOCK PICK KIT out of his pocket.

He stumbles to the entrance.

Sweating and out of breath.

Slowly realizing...

THE LOCK BOX IS GONE.

INT. BREAK ROOM - NIGHT

The CLOWN carries the LOCK BOX into a beige BREAK ROOM.

BRIGHT FLUORESCENTS. COOLERS. TABLES. MICROWAVE.

This is not the expected macabre Monster's lair from a glossy 2000s horror film. This is scary because it's NOT PRODUCTION DESIGNED. Just a very real, plain, forgettable break room that you would see at any make-shift construction site.

The CLOWN sits at a card table. Places the LOCK BOX in front of him. <u>Then REMOVES HIS MASK...</u>

INT. UNDERGROUND, TRAP DOOR - NIGHT

Nathan jolts awake. Takes stock of his new surroundings.

An empty cellar. A compartment in the ceiling from where he fell. Some PAINT CANS and TOOLS. Staircase twenty feet away.

INT. RED DOOR ROOM - NIGHT

Harper's RED KEY is BENDING, BENDING, BENDING, *WARPING, STRETCHING, BREAKING,* **BING!**

THE KEY SNAPS IN TWO.

Harper backs away from the door, terrified.

THE HANDLE UNLOCKS.

EXT. HAUNTED HOUSE - NIGHT

Evan sees the GHOST approaching outside.

>   EVAN
>   (afraid)
>   Where is everyone?

>   GHOST
>   Right behind me.

>   EVAN
>   (afraid)
>   Where's our phones?

>   GHOST
>   Someone's bringing them.

INT. BREAK ROOM - NIGHT

The CLOWN opens the LOCK BOX and spills the PHONES onto the table. <u>We do NOT see his face yet.</u>

He begins CLEARING EACH PHONE and RESTORING them to factory default. The phones that have a PASSCODE get placed in a separate pile.

The CLOWN grabs a phone we recognize as MALLORY'S. The screen now covered with a dozen congratulatory text messages: "OMG, you got the part!" "Break a leg!" He swipes the messages away with indifference and hits RESET. The phone goes dark.

INT. RED DOOR ROOM - NIGHT

Harper is paralyzed with fear. The RED DOOR slowly opens. The DEVIL steps inside.

Harper slinks to the ground. Curls up. Submissive. Afraid.

> HARPER
> Don't hurt me...
> I'm sorry...

The DEVIL stands over her, PITCH FORK raised to her head.

> HARPER
> Don't hurt me...
> Sam...

THE DEVIL SLOWLY REMOVES HIS MASK AND WE SEE THE SILHOUETTE OF A NIGHTMARE...

HIS FACE HIDEOUSLY DEFORMED BY EXTREME BODY MODIFICATION. RED SKIN. BLACK EYES. SHARP TEETH. POINTED EARS. THIS IS NOT A MASK - THIS IS A HUMAN FACE THAT RESEMBLES THE DEVIL.

> DEVIL
> WHO'S SAM?

INT. BREAK ROOM - NIGHT

A call comes through on Harper's iPHONE.

The CLOWN raises the PHONE to his head and we see his face for the first time:

SHAVED HEAD. WHITE AND RED CLOWN PAINT GREASED OVER HIS COMPLEXION. YELLOW EYES. ANIMAL FANGS DRILLED INTO HIS GUMS. PIN HOLES WHERE HIS EARS SHOULD BE.

(WE REALIZE: ALL OF THESE PEOPLE HAVE PAINSTAKINGLY MODIFIED THEIR FACES AND BODIES TO RESEMBLE MONSTERS)

> CLOWN
> (into phone)
> Hello?

> VOICE (V.O.)
> The fuck is this?

                    CLOWN
                (into phone)
            Who're you trying to reach?

The CLOWN's voice is completely average, a stark contrast to
his horrific face.

                    SAM (V.O.)
            Tell Harper her boyfriend Sam is
            coming for her.

                    CLOWN
                (into phone)
        ...

                    SAM (V.O.)
            Did you hear me? I said tell that
            fucking bitch she's dead.

                    CLOWN
                (into phone)
            Too late, Sam.

The CLOWN hangs up.

EXT. SAM'S PICKUP - NIGHT

Sam looks at his phone as the line goes dead. He narrows his
eyes. Jealous, angry, confused.

                                        BACK TO:

INT. BREAK ROOM - NIGHT

The CLOWN takes the pile of PHONES with PASSCODES and places
them in the MICROWAVE. He COOKS them.

(We may or may not notice he accidentally put Harper's phone
in the pile of "cleared phones".)

                    WITCH (O.S.)
            You strip her fingerprints?

The WITCH is standing in the doorway.

                    CLOWN
            Got someone working on it in the
            back. You on?

                         WITCH
               Nah. Traffic jam in Red Room.
                    (beat)
               Plans have changed.

The WITCH exits past a crudely-drawn BLUEPRINT MAP plastered
on the wall that outlines the entire haunted house. We push
in on a sketch labeled "Red Room"...

INT. RED DOOR ROOM - NIGHT

The DEVIL taps the pitchfork into Harper's cheek.

                         DEVIL
               Such a pretty mask.

                         HARPER
               I'm sorry...

Tears push out of Harper's eyes.

                         DEVIL
               Why don't we take it off. Find out
               who you really are.

THE BLACK CURTAIN OPENS.

The DEVIL turns. Nathan is on the other side of the fence.
He's holding a NAIL GUN. He aims it through the chain links --

CLINK CLINK CLINK!

The DEVIL shields himself from the assault.

The nails are fairly harmless at this range, but the
distraction gives Harper enough time to slip away.

                         NATHAN
               RUN HARPER!

Harper runs through the BLUE DOOR.

The DEVIL rams his PITCHFORK through the fence. Nathan
dodges.

EXT. HAUNTED HOUSE - NIGHT

It is unnaturally quiet outside the warehouse. Evan shivers.

                         EVAN
                    (afraid)
               They should've been out by now.

                         GHOST
            Do you still want to see my face?

                         EVAN
                    (afraid)
            What?

                         GHOST
            I was just wondering if you still
            wanted to see my face?

Evan notices the GHOST is holding a HAMMER.

                         EVAN
                    (afraid)
            I don't know. Whatever, it's fine.

                         GHOST
            Why not?

                         EVAN
                    (afraid)
            I just want to go home.

                         GHOST
            2425 Lincoln Road.

                         EVAN
            What?

A horrible moment as Evan realizes the GHOST just recited his
address from memory.

                         GHOST
            Because before, you were asking to
            see my face. So I just figured,
            maybe you still wanted to see it.
            It's a bit of a work-in-progress,
            but I think you might like it.

INT. RED DOOR ROOM - NIGHT

Nathan watches helplessly as the DEVIL pursues Harper through
the BLUE DOOR.

Nathan pushes open the TRICK DOOR in the wall that the WITCH
used earlier. It takes him to a HIDDEN PASSAGE behind the
scenes.

EXT. HAUNTED HOUSE - NIGHT

A GHOST **MASK** lays on the ground. Blood begins to pool around the pristine white plastic.

The mask is kicked out of view by a convulsing leg. Suddenly, the leg goes limp. Lifeless.

The GHOST pulls the claw of his HAMMER out of Evan's SKULL.

<u>**EVERY INCH OF THE GHOST'S FACE HAS BEEN TATTOOED THE COLOR OF ASH. THERE ARE TRIANGULAR SKELETAL HOLES WHERE NOSE CARTILAGE SHOULD BE. CHEEKBONES SHAVED AND SUNKEN. NO TEETH - THEY'VE ALL BEEN REMOVED. CRACKED LIPS, DRY AND FLAKY. ETHEREAL WISPS OF BLACK HAIR HANG SHOULDER LENGTH.**</u>

The GHOST begins to peel Evan's face off with the hammer claw.

INT. BLACK CORRIDOR - NIGHT

Harper runs into the fog. Passes the ghost-like BODIES DRAPED IN WHITE CLOTH that Nathan saw earlier.

INT. STAIRS - NIGHT

She climbs a narrow staircase.

INT. TILTED HALL - NIGHT

The staircase lands in a SLANTED HALL that seems to extend into infinity, where the floor is diagonal, and the dimensions of the walls and ceiling are angled out of proportion.

It gives Harper a feeling of vertigo that is abstract and suffocating.

Harper stumbles through the canted hallway.

THERE'S A CLOSED DOOR halfway through, about twenty feet away.

It RATTLES loudly throughout the angled corridor.

Harper runs past the door.

The seemingly endless hall abruptly bottlenecks to a DEAD END - <u>the length was just an illusion created by FORCED PERSPECTIVE</u>.

Above the DEAD END, a PLASTIC BUCKET hangs by a rope from the ceiling. It appears to be filled with dozens of FLASHLIGHTS.

BEHIND HER, THE DOOR BEGINS TO SHAKE VIOLENTLY.

Harper reaches into the bucket and grabs a BLACK MAG-LITE.

AS SOON AS THE WEIGHT OF THE MAG-LITE IS REMOVED, THE BUCKET ascends into the ceiling which makes THE LIGHTS CUT OUT.

                              HARPER
              Shit.

Harper turns on the FLASHLIGHT. The beam cuts a small window in the darkness. She sees --

THE DOOR STOPS RATTLING.

THE DOOR KNOB TURNS.

THE DOOR SLOWLY CREEPS OPEN...

INT. HIDDEN PASSAGE - NIGHT

Nathan moves stealthily behind the scenes of the house.

There are taped cables, switchboards, crude markers. It's akin to being backstage at a playhouse.

His foot kicks something SHINY --

It's the MOONSTONE RING. The ring Bailey lost, the one that belongs to Harper's mother.

Nathan realizes he's on the other side of the "Guess the Body Parts" wall.

INT. BREAK ROOM - NIGHT

Nathan ducks into the BREAK ROOM. It's empty now. He takes the space in, curious.

Quickly spots Harper's iPHONE on the card table next to the open LOCK BOX. *Thank God.*

Nathan sneaks over to the PHONE, but...

HE HEARS SOMEONE COMING.

Nathan backtracks, hides behind a loose SHEET OF TARP hanging off the wall.

His face glows a dark blue. Sweat trickles down his forehead. He stifles his breathing under the palm of his hand.

He cannot see who is in the break room with him. <u>He can only HEAR them</u>.

INT. TILTED HALL - NIGHT

Harper approaches the OPENED DOOR with her flashlight.

No one's there. She steps inside...

INT. BLACKOUT ROOM - NIGHT

Harper doesn't notice the door mechanically shut and lock behind her. <u>That's because it's impossible to see anything in this room</u>. The walls have been painted black. And the only light comes from the dim bulb of Harper's FLASHLIGHT.

Harper cautiously moves forward.

The narrow beam reveals a row of NAILS upturned on the floor. She carefully steps around them.

She pans the flashlight left, sees KNIVES dangling from the ceiling. Harper ducks under them.

Ahead, BEAR TRAPS and SNARES fade into darkness all around.

Harper realizes...

<u>EVERY INCH OF THIS ROOM HAS BEEN CAREFULLY DESIGNED TO HURT.</u>

But that's not the worst part. The worst part...

Harper's flashlight was loaded with DEAD BATTERIES. Which means she's going to have to walk through this room in the dark. Because her flashlight is starting to **DIE** --

> HARPER
> -- no, please.

INT. BREAK ROOM - NIGHT

Nathan is still hiding behind the blue tarp. He hears items being knocked around a table.

He tries to wipe sweat from his forehead, but accidentally RUSTLES the tarp.

<u>The items on the table suddenly go silent.</u>

A figure approaches and stops just inches away from Nathan.

There's a long moment of dead silence, before...

The figure retreats from the tarp. We hear footsteps, growing further and further away...

The room falls completely quiet.

Nathan takes a breath, relieved. It's safe. He steps out from the tarp to find --

-- the GHOST stands on the opposite side of the room. His MASK back on.

Neither the GHOST nor Nathan say a word. They hold eye contact, unsure of each other's next move.

>   NATHAN
>   Where are my friends?

The GHOST says nothing.

>   NATHAN
>   Mitch, I need to know they're okay.

Nathan steps towards the table...

>   NATHAN
>   Can you tell me where they are?

Nathan grabs the phone...

>   GHOST
>   Put that phone to your head and
>   I'll kill you.

Nathan freezes. Makes his gestures as inconspicuous as possible as he talks --

>   NATHAN
>   Okay okay okay, I don't want that
>   to happen. I'm not gonna do that...

Nathan opens a text thread with the last dialed number. There's a message that says "I SEE YOU".

>   NATHAN
>   ...I just want to make sure we're
>   cool, all right? And that my
>   friends...

Quickly, Nathan drops a GPS pin and texts "HELP" to the last number called (i.e. SAM).

                         NATHAN
                ...I wanna make sure they're still
                alive, okay?

SWOOSH. The outgoing text makes a noise <u>RIGHT AS</u> --

The GHOST slaps the phone out of Nathan's hand and swings a
HAMMER at his head. He whiffs. Nathan pushes him over and
runs back the way he came.

EXT. HIGHWAY ROAD - NIGHT

Sam is driving. His phone is on the dashboard of his truck. A
TEXT comes in that says "HELP".

INT. BLACKOUT ROOM - NIGHT

HARPER'S FLASHLIGHT IS FLICKERING UNCONTROLLABLY.

She SMACKS it, giving her a fleeting view of the room that
expires after a millisecond.

BLACKOUT.

She SMACKS it again. The light strobes, then holds steady.

She takes a few steps forward.

BLACKOUT.

Back on. A few more steps.

BLACKOUT.

                         HARPER
                ...please...

Back on. Her face comes within inches of a DEADLY SERRATED
BLADE. She sidesteps and continues.

BLACKOUT.

Back on. A series of hanging KNIVES are swinging, as if
someone just passed by.

FOOTSTEPS RETREAT INTO THE SHADOWS.

HARPER IS NOT ALONE.

BLACKOUT.

Harper's waning light desperately searches the room.
Whoever's there is just outside the light's reach...

                         HARPER
          ...hello?

BLACKOUT.

Back on. She catches a glimpse of an APPROACHING FIGURE --

Harper recoils, steps back and --

SHE SCREAMS AS HER FOOT PIERCES A NAIL!

BLACKOUT.

INT. BACK ROOM - NIGHT

Someone in a GRIM REAPER MASK reacts to the SCREAM. They are
seated in an empty back room. The CLOWN and WITCH move around
in the foreground.

The REAPER's arms and legs are covered by a long BLACK HOODED
CLOAK. There's something ominous about his demeanor, as he
simply sits and waits. Listening...

INT. HIDDEN PASSAGE - NIGHT

Nathan sneaks around behind the scenes, careful not to get
caught.

He comes across a LADDER that leads to a HATCH in the
ceiling.

EXT. HAUNTED HOUSE, HATCH - NIGHT

Nathan climbs through the hatch.

                         NATHAN
          Holy shit.

He is OUTSIDE the haunted house. The welcoming sound of
cicadas all around him. An icy fall breeze on his face. The
parking lot less than a baseball field away.

But Nathan is hit with a pang of guilt. Leave his friends
behind or die trying to save them? Go for the easy line drive
or swing fearlessly into the pitch?

Nathan starts making his way toward the parking lot. Playing
it safe, just like always.

INT. BLACKOUT ROOM - NIGHT

Harper's light comes back on. She pries her foot from the nail and cradles the wound, examining her next move.

On the far side of the wall is a SMALL PASSAGEWAY - the only way out of this room.

BLACKOUT.

Back on. Her light catches something shiny suspended above the passageway...

A GUILLOTINE BLADE hangs from the ceiling by way of a LONG ROPE. And if it falls, the blade will block her only exit.

With her light, she traces the rope's origins --

BLACKOUT.

Back on. The rope is threaded along the ceiling, bending downwards on the far opposite wall where --

BLACKOUT.

Back on. Harper gasps. Twenty feet away, the VAMPIRE is cutting the rope with a MACHETE. If it drops, Harper will be trapped inside.

Harper crawls towards the passage on her hands and knees.

Through BROKEN GLASS and other SHARP OBJECTS.

BLACKOUT.

Back on. She notices a CLEAR RESIDUE on the floor all around her. It's holding her hands and legs in place.

BLACKOUT.

Harper tries to pull her hands and legs out of the INDUSTRIAL STRENGTH ADHESIVE coating the floor, but the glue has already bonded.

BLACKOUT.

Back on. Harper's skin gruesomely PEELS OFF on the floor as she quickly tries to move.

The VAMPIRE cuts the rope. Harper SCREAMS. The GUILLOTINE FALLS. HARPER JUMPS THROUGH JUST IN TIME.

INT. BLACKOUT ROOM, PASSAGE - NIGHT

Harper sprints ahead. Her legs give out because of panic and she hits the ground. She pushes herself up painfully with her raw blistered hands.

Harper comes to a door labeled: ESCAPE ROOM.

INT. LITTLE GIRL'S BEDROOM - NIGHT

Harper enters the ESCAPE ROOM, throws the door shut, sees --

DOLLS. PINK WALLPAPER. VANITY MIRRORS. OAK DRESSER. A PRINCESS BED IN THE CORNER.

-- this room has been designed to resemble a little girl's bedroom.

Harper immediately pushes the heavy OAK DRESSER in front of the door, sealing it shut. She notices...

SOMETHING WRITTEN ON THE WALL WHERE THE DRESSER USED TO BE:

ESU⬤H ⬤ETNUⴄH EHT EPⴄƆSE ⬤T YEK EHT ⬤NIꟻ

The letters seem scrambled. Harper takes out her RED COMPACT MIRROR and holds it up to the writing:

FIN⬤ THE KEY T⬤ ESƆⴄPE THE HⴄUNTE⬤ H⬤USE

Harper moves to the FLORAL PATTERNED DOOR on the far wall. It's LOCKED, but is spray-painted with a message: THE END. There's a large dungeon style KEYHOLE. She tries the various keys on her KEY-RING, but none of them fit. <u>She needs to find the key that unlocks the floral door</u>.

> HARPER
> (thinking)
> ...key, uh...

Harper searches all of the dresser drawers. Each drawer is empty. She opens the last one...

Inside is a square piece of WALLPAPER. Same pink pattern that can be seen all around the room. What does it mean?

Harper studies the walls. Looking for any imperfections or anomalies. Finds a corner that's starting to peel...

She rips down the peeling section of wallpaper. A second message written underneath:

LLA EES SLLOD

She translates the scrambled text with her COMPACT MIRROR:

DOLLS SEE ALL

                    HARPER
                  (thinking)
            ...dolls...

Harper knocks over the bin of VINTAGE DOLLS. The dolls spill to the floor. They are large, with black eyes, androgynous features. Creepy enough to be cousins of Annabelle.

Harper undresses the dolls, looking for the next clue, but finds nothing. She glances around, unsure.

Gets an idea...

Harper snaps one of the DOLL'S heads. Underneath its broken porcelain EYES, a third and final message:

DEI EHT REDNU GNIDIH SI GNIHTEMOS

Harper's hands shake as she holds up the mirror. What she sees makes her blood run cold.

SOMETHING IS HIDING UNDER THE BED

Harper paces. Resigned to the inevitable.

                    HARPER
                (breathing heavy)
            ...

She takes a few conservative steps towards the PRINCESS BED.

Glances below. It is completely dark underneath. She doesn't have the nerve to look closer.

She slowly peels back the comforter revealing BLOOD STAINED BEDSHEETS.

Harper is frozen in fear. This is all wrong.

Harper leans onto the bed, feeling the pillow-top mattress through the crimson soaked sheets. Searching for a key.

There's a loud CREAK underneath the bed. Harper gets very still. She listens. Did she make that sound?

ANOTHER CREAK.

A chill runs down Harper's spine. Couldn't have been her. She kneels - VERY VERY VERY SLOWLY - to peer underneath the bed.

SILENCE.

Her head is all the way passed the frame now. She places her cheek to the floor. Looks into darkness...

CAN'T SEE ANYTHING.

Harper begins a slow crawl under the frame.

FLASH CUT: Young Harper crawls under her bed, afraid.

Her eyes adjusting.

There's a small ornate BOX against the wall. A HANDLE sticks out from the side.

Harper is completely under the bed now. She lifts the box and turns the handle.

THE BOX PRODUCES AN EERIE STACCATO MELODY.

Harper's eyes narrow.

The music and rotating handle wind down to a stop.

Harper blinks.

The thick stillness of silence is interrupted by the *SUDDEN POP OF THE BOX* --

Harper stifles a SCREAM.

A **JACK IN THE BOX** bobs on a spring. It holds a CAST IRON KEY.

                    HARPER
                  (exhales)
          ...jesus.

Harper takes a breath. She pries the KEY from the Jack in the Box.

JUST THEN THE OAK DRESSER (THAT'S HOLDING THE DOOR SHUT) STARTS TO RATTLE.

Harper turns.

THUD. THE DRESSER IS HIT WITH GREAT FORCE FROM THE OTHER SIDE. IT SLIDES A QUARTER OF AN INCH.

                    HARPER
          ...no no no...

THUD. THE DRESSER MOVES AGAIN. SOMEONE IS FORCING THEIR WAY THROUGH THE DOOR.

Harper curls up, sliding under the bed, terrified.

ANOTHER THUD ECHOES THROUGH THE ROOM. THE OAK DRESSER TOPPLES OVER AS THE DOOR IS PUSHED OPEN.

A long shadow enters.

The shadow slinks past the bed.

HARPER CLOSES HER EYES, PRAYING THE SHADOW DISAPPEARS.

> MALE VOICE (O.S.)
> Thought I told you to clean up.

HER EYES OPEN, STRUCK BY THE FAMILIAR VOICE. We see a pair of WORK BOOTS hover near the scattered DOLLS.

> MALE VOICE (O.S.)
> Harper. I'm talking to you.

Harper covers her mouth. Doesn't respond.

SOMETHING DROPS ONTO THE FLOOR AND ROLLS UNDER THE BED.

Harper watches a BEER BOTTLE come to a stop right next to her face.

> MALE VOICE (O.S.)
> I'm sorry about what happened
> earlier. Mommy's fine.
> (beat)
> Do you forgive Daddy?

It's hard to tell if this is dream, or memory, or something else entirely... but the VOICE belongs to HARPER'S FATHER.

> HARPER
> (tears)
> ...yes...

> HARPER'S FATHER (O.S.)
> Why don't you come out from under
> there?

> HARPER
> (tears)
> ...okay...

Harper is reeling. Tears fill her eyes. She seems to be re-living a repressed memory from her abusive childhood.

                    HARPER'S FATHER (O.S.)
              I just really care --

                    SAM (O.S.)
              -- about you.

Her father's voice turns into SAM'S VOICE.

                    SAM (O.S.)
              You know I get self-conscious
              sometimes...
                    (beat)
              When you...

The shadow moves over to the PRINCESS BED. The WORK BOOTS are
now SAM'S SNEAKERS.

                    SAM (O.S.)
              When you talk to other guys.

HARPER CLOSES HER EYES AGAIN.

                    HARPER
              I know...
              I'm sorry...

SAM'S SNEAKERS are now a RED GOWN. We realize the DEVIL has
been in the room this entire time. HARPER IS HALLUCINATING.

*FLASH CUT: Young Harper hiding under her bed, her face red
from crying.*

                    NATHAN (V.O.)
              Nothing scary ever happened to you?

                    HARPER (V.O.)
              We were happy.

*FLASH CUT: Harper's FATHER hitting Harper's Mother. A RING
flies off her finger and tumbles under the bed.*

                    BAILEY (V.O.)
              Tell me a story about why you're
              sad.

*FLASH CUT: Harper and Sam argue. He's been drinking. Sam
punches Harper under the eye, causing a BRUISE to form.*

                    HARPER (V.O.)
              Do you think I'm sad?

AN OVERWHELMING CACOPHONY OF VOICES AND IMAGES BEGIN TO FLOOD
HARPER'S SUBCONSCIOUS; REPRESSED MEMORIES THAT SHE HAS BEEN
HIDING UNDER A **MASK** HER ENTIRE LIFE.

> HARPER (V.O.)
> I grew up in a haunted house.

Harper clenches her fist around the CAST IRON KEY. Her
breathing intensifies. Her face tightens. And then...

> BAILEY (V.O.)
> But the story has a happy ending...
> (beat)
> ...you got out.

Her eyes snap open. The hallucinations and voices are gone.
The DEVIL kneels at the edge of the bed. His body inches
away.

> DEVIL (O.S.)
> Come out.

A calm washes over Harper's face. Her body relaxes. Something
about her is different. Something that is going to change
everything.

> DEVIL (O.S.)
> Let's take off your mask.

The DEVIL's demonic eyes peer under the bed, scanning the
darkness, searching for --

> HARPER
> **NO!**

HARPER PLUNGES THE CAST-IRON KEY INTO THE DEVIL'S EYE SOCKET.

THE DEVIL LETS OUT A SHRILL WAIL. FLIES ACROSS THE ROOM.
WRITHES ON THE FLOOR. HIS FACE TWISTING IN AGONY AS --

Harper slides out from the bed. She runs to the FLORAL
PATTERNED DOOR and inserts the KEY.

SHE TURNS THE KEY ONCE. TWICE. THREE TIMES... THE KEY CLICKS.

> HARPER
> Come on, come on.

THE EERIE STACCATO MELODY BOOMS LOUDLY THROUGHOUT THE ROOM.

AS THE MUSIC PLAYS, THE KEY ROTATES LIKE A GEAR. SLOWLY
WINDING DOWN JUST LIKE THE HANDLE ON THE JACK IN THE BOX.

Harper backs away from the door in anticipation of what's
behind.

Nearby, the DEVIL squirms in a pool of his own blood.

                    DEVIL
            MY EYE MY FUCKING EYE

THE STACCATO MELODY SLOWS TO A STOP.

DEAD SILENCE.

...

  . . .

      ● ● ●

BOOM! THE FLORAL DOOR EXPLODES IN A BLAST OF BUCKSHOT.

HARPER JUMPS. TAKES A HIT IN THE SHOULDER. FALLS.

THE SHOTGUN BLAST CAME FROM BEHIND THE DOOR.

EXT. HAUNTED HOUSE, PARKING LOT - NIGHT

Nathan is halfway across the parking lot when he hears the
GUNSHOT. He stops and listens.

EXT. HIGHWAY ROAD - NIGHT

Sam SLAMS on the brakes. His red pickup skids to a halt. He
heard the gunshot too. Stares out the window at a dense
forest. Looks back to his dash where his phone is navigating
him to the GPS PIN DROP Nathan texted...

INT. LITTLE GIRL'S BEDROOM - NIGHT

THE STACCATO MELODY RESETS AND PLAYS AGAIN.

HARPER LOOKS INTO A SPLINTERED PORTAL OF WOOD AND FLOATING
DEBRIS. DOESN'T SEE ANYONE ON THE OTHER SIDE.

THE DEVIL GRABS HER FROM BEHIND.

SHE MANEUVERS AWAY.

HARPER CRAWLS THROUGH THE BROKEN PIECES OF FLORAL DOOR INTO --

INT. DARK HALL - NIGHT

-- A DARK HALL. Her shoulder leaves a small trail of BLOOD.

THE MUSIC SLOWS TO A STOP.

...

. . .

• • •

BOOM! RIGHT ON CUE - A SHOTGUN MUZZLE FLASH LIGHTS THE HALL. FOR A FLEETING SECOND WE SEE THE GUN IS RIGGED TO A WALL TWENTY FEET AWAY.

HARPER DODGES THE SPRAY. KEEPS CRAWLING TOWARDS THE FIREARM.

THE DEVIL GRABS HARPER'S WOUNDED SHOULDER.

HARPER SCREAMS.

THE MELODY RESETS AND PLAYS AGAIN.

HARPER TRIES TO FIGHT BACK.

THE DEVIL THROWS HARPER DOWN.

HE HITS HER ACROSS THE FACE.

THE MUSIC SLOWS TO A STOP.

...

HARPER PUTS PRESSURE ON THE DEVIL'S WOUNDED EYE.

. . .

THE DEVIL RECOILS IN PAIN, DRAWING HIS HEAD BACK.

• • •

HARPER PUSHES THE DEVIL UP --

BOOM! THE DEVIL'S SKULL COMES APART IN A THIRD SHOTGUN BLAST. HIS HEADLESS BODY BUCKLES AND FALLS.

THE MELODY RESETS AND PLAYS AGAIN.

HARPER PUSHES THE DEVIL'S CORPSE AWAY AND STAGGERS TOWARDS THE SHOTGUN AS FAST AS SHE CAN.

THE MUSIC SLOWS TO A STOP.

...

HARPER'S TEN FEET AWAY.

. . .

FIVE FEET.

. . .

ONE.

. . .

CLICK! THE GUN IS OUT OF AMMO, THANK FUCKING GOD! HARPER
FALLS OVER, RELIEVED, GRATEFUL!

We see the shotgun is rigged to a ROTARY DEVICE that spins as
the music plays, which eventually activates the trigger.

Harper tries to wrestle the weapon away from its perch, but
it's no use.

As she looks around for what's ahead, Harper quickly
realizes...

INT. END OF HAUNTED HOUSE - NIGHT

...this is what everything has been leading to. A fucking
empty plywood wall. A dead end. A TRAP. THERE IS NO EXIT.

EXT. HAUNTED HOUSE, PARKING LOT - NIGHT

The CLOWN stands outside Evan's car. The doors are locked. He
swings a SLEDGEHAMMER through the driver's side window.

He unlocks the door and gets inside. Rifles through the dash,
glove box, looking for keys. NOTHING.

INT. BODY ROOM - NIGHT

The CLOWN arrives at the BODY ROOM, which is occupied by a
few others. A row of TRASH BINS line the wall. Recently
purchased boxes from the chainsaw, props, decorations
scattered about.

                    CLOWN
          Alright let's dump the trash and
          get out of here.

                         VAMPIRE
              Who's making the oil run?

                         CLOWN
              We're not there yet. One thing at a
              time.

                         VAMPIRE
                    (re: trash bins)
              Prints are gone. Clipped fingers
              and toes. Dental is bagged.

                         CLOWN
              You find keys?

                         VAMPIRE
              Keys?

                         CLOWN
              On any of the bodies. There's a car
              out front I still gotta move.

                         VAMPIRE
              Fuck, forgot to look.

The CLOWN shakes his head, annoyed.

                         CLOWN
              That's not all you forgot.

He holds the RECEIPT that Evan discovered in the Spider Room.

                         CLOWN
              Has the time stamp on it. If
              forensics found this, they'd pull
              security tape from the store, have
              you ID'd, then come after all of
              us.
                    (beat)
              So start doing your fucking job.

The VAMPIRE nods, nervously. He moves to the first TRASH BIN.
Flips open the top: inside is a BLACK BODY BAG. He unzips the
body bag and searches the CORPSE for KEYS.

The GHOST enters, frantic.

                         GHOST
                    (urgent)
              What's going on?

                         CLOWN
              Martinis. Packing up.

                        GHOST
          One of them got out.

                        CLOWN
          Nah, the shotty got him. Didn't you
          hear it?

                        GHOST
          No, one of them got out <u>backstage</u>.

                        CLOWN
          Fuck, when was this?

                        GHOST
          What if he got outside?

                        CLOWN
          He didn't get outside.

                        GHOST
          But what if he did?

The CLOWN considers the bad news. Mind racing.

He sees the GRIM REAPER sitting silently in an adjacent room.

                        CLOWN
          He didn't. Send the Reaper through.
          He'll draw them out. We'll know if
          anyone's still knocking around
          inside.
                    (pointing to others)
          Everyone else, sweep backstage.

The GHOST approaches the GRIM REAPER.

                        GHOST
          Ready?

The GRIM REAPER stands. He is led through a TRICK DOOR in the
wall.

                        GHOST
          Just walk straight through, and
          then we can all go home.

The CLOWN picks up his SLEDGEHAMMER. Walks to a BREAKER on
the wall, throws a switch --

ALL THE LIGHTS IN THE HAUNTED HOUSE TURN ON.

                        CLOWN
          Last looks.

INT. BLACK CORRIDOR - NIGHT

The haunted house is less scary with the lights on. But
there's something eerie still about the GRIM REAPER: the way
he moves, deliberately taking in his surroundings with a
vacant gaze.

The GRIM REAPER passes through the black corridor...

All the fog has dissipated...

INT. STAIRS - NIGHT

Climbs the narrow staircase...

No music now, just silence...

INT. TILTED HALL - NIGHT

Along the tilted hallway...

The illusion of forced perspective undermined in the light.
Now it's just another hallway...

INT. BLACKOUT ROOM - NIGHT

Inside the blackout room...

All the traps and snares visible, unthreatening...

INT. LITTLE GIRL'S BEDROOM - NIGHT

Arrives at the escape room. He turns the corner into the
final dark corridor and...

INT. END OF HAUNTED HOUSE - NIGHT

...*holy fucking shit... look at all that blood... what the
fuck happened here... blood everywhere... BAM!*

THE GRIM REAPER IS HIT FROM BEHIND BY HARPER, WHO WAS HIDING
UNDER THE PRINCESS BED.

THE GRIM REAPER TUMBLES OVER, EASILY. ALMOST TOO EASILY.
HARPER DRIVES THE PITCH FORK INTO THE REAPER'S CHEST, PINNING
HIM TO THE GROUND.

THE GRIM REAPER SQUIRMS. A MUFFLED SCREAM MURMURS FROM BEHIND
THE MASK, SUPPRESSED BY SOMETHING STRONGER THAN PRIDE.

HARPER PEELS BACK THE REAPER'S MASK, AND SEES --

the worst thing imaginable

-- BAILEY'S TERRIFIED BLEEDING FACE, BRUISED AND BROKEN. DUCT TAPE PLASTERED ACROSS HER MOUTH. AS HARPER PEELS BACK THE BLACK GOWN BAILEY HAS BEEN COVERED WITH, SHE FINDS HER FRIEND'S ARMS TIED BEHIND HER BACK WITH ZIP TIES. BAILEY WAS USED AS BAIT.

> HARPER
> NO NO NO NO

The sound fades away. Harper sobs, clutching onto Bailey. She tears the duct tape. Cradles her friend's face. We hear...

> BAILEY
> ...they're coming for you...

Louder.

> BAILEY
> ...they're coming for you...

LOUDER.

> BAILEY
> ...they're coming for you...

EVERYTHING IN HER LUNGS, THE LAST BREATH BAILEY WILL EVER TAKE.

> BAILEY
> THEY'RE COMING FOR YOU, RUN!

EXT. HIGHWAY ROAD - NIGHT

An eerie silence sets in. Crickets. A cool breeze. The subtle DING of an open car door...

SAM'S RED PICKUP is parked on the side of the road.

INT. HAUNT, BACKSTAGE STORAGE - NIGHT

A heavy iron door is hit from the other side. It bursts open.

Sam steps inside. Takes in his surroundings. He's behind the scenes of the haunted house. Boxes of Halloween decorations in the corner. Discarded power tools on the floor.

He checks his phone, closing in on the PIN DROP that was
texted to him earlier.

INT. HAUNT, BACKSTAGE HALL - NIGHT

Sam turns a corner. Passes an EXPOSED PIPE protruding from
the wall. Steam HISSES out of the pipe and for a moment it
catches Sam's attention until he sees...

A figure at the end of a long hall. The Clown.

Sam approaches, cautiously. He doesn't want to get caught.
But he's curious...

                    SAM
          Hello?

The Clown doesn't respond. Sam gets closer.

                    SAM
          Hey, I'm looking for someone.

Closer still. No response.

                    SAM
          I said I'm looking for --

SNAP!!! SAM STEPS THROUGH AN ORANGE TRIPWIRE --

THE WIRE PLUCKS A 2-INCH ROD FROM A HIDDEN MECHANISM --

THE ROD SPINS IN THE AIR AS --

A PROJECTILE ROCKETS OUT OF THE EXPOSED PIPE --

THE ROD HITS THE FLOOR --

IN A MATTER OF SECONDS -- *THUNK* -- A RUSTED BOLT CUTS INTO
THE BACK OF SAM'S NECK.

The Clown, hearing the trap, turns to find Sam.

Sam drops to his knees. His PHONE flies forward. Not sure
what hit him. A trickle of blood rolls down his throat. He
sucks in air, trying to breathe, but can't.

He falls over. Dying. Reaching for his phone.

The Clown approaches. Picks up a nearby CINDERBLOCK.

Sam coughs blood. Pulls the BOLT out of his throat. Still
reaching for his phone. Mumbles...

                         SAM
          ...help.

The Clown drops the CINDER BLOCK on Sam's hand, crushing it
instantly. Sam tries to scream but can't. Blood pouring out
of his throat now.

The Clown picks up another CINDER BLOCK and drops it on Sam's
legs. Then another. Drops it on Sam's back. <u>Sam is completely
pinned in place under the weight of the cinder blcoks</u>.

The Clown picks up his SLEDGEHAMMER. In no hurry. Settles on
Sam's desperate gaze. As he tees up a golf swing straight
into Sam's face -- SMASH!

                                             BACK TO:

INT. END OF HAUNTED HOUSE - NIGHT

Harper desperately backs away from Bailey in shock and
despair. Her hand covers her mouth, unable to comprehend.

Things are about to get very bad.

Brum-BRUMMMMMMMMMMMMMMMMMMMM!!

The chainsaw roars nearby, moving steadily through the Little
Girl's Bedroom, drawing closer.

Harper backs up against the plywood dead end. Steels herself.
Prepares for what's next. She can't even scream.

THE HEAD OF A SLEDGEHAMMER COMES THROUGH THE WALL, NARROWLY
MISSING THE BACK OF HARPER'S HEAD.

SHE RECOILS IN TERROR. FALLS TO HER KNEES. TURNS.

THE SLEDGEHAMMER STRIKES AGAIN. HACKING THROUGH IN LONG,
MENACING STRIDES. AS IF HUNTING FOR SOMEONE. AS IF SEARCHING
FOR --

                         NATHAN
          HARPER!

Nathan peers through the thin puncture hole he cut from the
wall. Harper jumps to her feet, relieved.

                         HARPER
          Nathan. Someone's. Coming.

INT. HIDDEN PASSAGE, WALL - NIGHT

We briefly see the other side of the wall that separates
them: The CLOWN lies in a pool of his own blood. His arm <u>has
been smashed and twisted back</u>, broken by the sledgehammer.
Nathan <u>doesn't</u> see the CLOWN slowly crawling to safety.

                    NATHAN
          Gonna get you out, back up.

INT. END OF HAUNTED HOUSE - NIGHT

Harper backs away as Nathan continues chipping at the wall.

The ZOMBIE enters. He drags his CHAINSAW along the walls, and
Harper realizes this time <u>it's real</u>, as sparks and sawdust
fly everywhere.

Harper thinks fast. She looks at the tethered shotgun.
Searches the platform it sits upon, finds...

A BOX OF SHOTGUN SHELLS HIDDEN UNDERNEATH.

She grabs a shell and tries to load the gun. It's not that
simple. Harper has never used a weapon before. Doesn't know
what to do.

INT. HIDDEN PASSAGE, WALL - NIGHT

Nathan takes a hard swing and the sledge gets STUCK. He puts
a foot on the wall for leverage. Pulls as hard as he can.

A FLOORBOARD BEHIND HIM CREAKS. <u>IT'S THE GHOST</u>.

Nathan jumps. The sledge comes flying out of the wall. The
inertia forces Nathan off balance as the GHOST throws him to
the ground. <u>The sledgehammer lands out of reach</u>.

Nearby, the CLOWN escapes unseen.

INT. END OF HAUNTED HOUSE - NIGHT

The ZOMBIE realizes Harper is trying to load the shotgun. He
runs at her.

Harper, desperate, pulls back the pump. <u>It locks</u>. Progress?
She's not sure. Notices the ZOMBIE, *fuck, um, um, okay, um...*

Harper pushes the SHELL into the ejection port which isn't
really the proper way to load a shotgun, but she wouldn't
know that, and it'll still get the job done.

She racks back the pump, fingers the trigger, starts to
squeeze --

TOO LATE. The ZOMBIE swings the chainsaw at her. But unlike
their first encounter, Harper fights back! She dodges the saw
and locks arms with the ZOMBIE.

They struggle a moment. The saw getting closer to her face.

INT. HIDDEN PASSAGE, WALL - NIGHT

On the other side of the wall, the GHOST has Nathan pinned.
He punches him hard. Knocks the wind out of his lungs. Spits
in his face.

                    GHOST
          Want to know my name?

The GHOST strangles Nathan. His face turns red. Tears well in
his eyes. As he starts to die...

INT. END OF HAUNTED HOUSE - NIGHT

Harper shoves the saw away. The blade comes down on the
BARREL OF THE SHOTGUN, SAWING IT RIGHT OFF IN ONE FELL SWOOP.

The shotgun is now a SAWED-OFF SHOTGUN.

HARPER RELEASES THE SAW, REACHES FOR THE TRIGGER, SQUEEZES
BOOOOOOOOOOOOM THE GUN BACKFIRES FROM THE SAWED BARREL. FIERY
SHARDS OF METAL EXPLODE IN THE ZOMBIE'S FACE, KNOCKING HIM
BACK, GIVING HARPER JUST ENOUGH TIME TO RUN TO THE WALL --

But the hole isn't big enough to crawl through. Harper rips
at the splintered plywood, pulling it apart with her bleeding
hands, MAKING THE HOLE BIG ENOUGH TO SQUEEZE INSIDE.

INT. HIDDEN PASSAGE, WALL - NIGHT

Harper picks up the SLEDGEHAMMER. Heavier than she thought.
She stumbles, off balance. Races to Nathan. Winds up and...

THUD! LANDS A FATAL BLOW TO THE BACK OF THE GHOST'S NECK.

Nathan staggers to his feet, catches his breath.

                    NATHAN
                 (no voice)
          This way.

INT. HIDDEN PASSAGE - NIGHT

Harper sees Sam's body. A bloody mangled mess. She can't possibly comprehend what happened to him.

INT. BLACK CORRIDOR - NIGHT

The CLOWN limps through the house, losing a lot of blood. Scared. Grappling with his own mortality for the first time.

INT. HIDDEN PASSAGE - NIGHT

Harper and Nathan turn a corner, find the VAMPIRE with his arms up. He drops a MACHETE to the ground.

>   VAMPIRE
>   (scared)
>   I didn't kill anyone. I was just
>   helping out, I'm sorry.

Harper grips the SLEDGE, not sure what to do.

The VAMPIRE flips his mask, revealing --

A YOUNG MAN (LATE 20s). HIS FACE IS COMPLETELY NORMAL, UNMARRED BY BODY MODIFICATIONS LIKE THE OTHERS. NO PIERCINGS, NO TATTOOS, JUST A NERVOUS MAN CONSUMED BY FEAR.

>   VAMPIRE
>   (scared)
>   I wanna go back to prison.

Harper and Nathan lock eyes.

INT. BREAK ROOM - NIGHT

The VAMPIRE walks ahead of Harper and Nathan, hands still above his head. Nathan now holds the MACHETE.

>   VAMPIRE
>   (sobbing)
>   This is so fucked up. They didn't
>   tell me it was gonna be real. I
>   thought, sure, we'll mess with some
>   kids, but then they started killing
>   them -

>   NATHAN
>   Shhh.

                    VAMPIRE
          - they said if I killed someone,
          I'd earn my face.

In a plea, the Vampire looks back at Nathan and Harper.

                    NATHAN
          Turn around.

                    VAMPIRE
          I'm just their errands guy. I buy
          the shit for them. That's it.

                    NATHAN
          Turn around.

                    VAMPIRE
          We can go to the cops. I don't know
          their names, but I can track them
          down. One of them works at a tattoo
          shop, one of them's a dealer, we
          can find these guys. They said they
          did this another time, in Tulsa or
          Texas, I forget, but we can stop
          them.

They enter the break room. It's empty.

                    VAMPIRE
               (sobbing)
          I'm so sorry.

INT. HIDDEN PASSAGE, HATCH - NIGHT

Nathan leads them to the exit LADDER. Everyone does their
best not to make a sound.

The VAMPIRE recognizes where they are. He immediately starts
rummaging through a panel in the wall.

                    NATHAN
               (hushed)
          Hey! Stop that!

He's making a lot of NOISE, digging for something.

                    NATHAN
               (hushed)
          Hey! Stop!

                    VAMPIRE
          It's fine, it's fine.

                    NATHAN
                 (hushed)
          Stop! What're you doing?!

                    VAMPIRE
          It's fine, I know where they hide a
          gun.

                    NATHAN
                 (hushed)
          Forget it, let's go!

                    VAMPIRE
          That's weird, it used to be right
          here --

CRACK! THE VAMPIRE'S HEAD EXPLODES FROM A GUNSHOT. HE
CRUMPLES, BLOOD SPURTING FROM THE EXIT WOUND.

HARPER SCREAMS. DROPS THE SLEDGEHAMMER.

NATHAN, SPATTERED WITH BLOOD, TURNS TO SEE THE ZOMBIE HIDING
IN THE SHADOWS. THE ZOMBIE RAISES A .38 TO HARPER'S HEAD.

WE GLIMPSE HIS CRUMBLING FACE, OOZING AND PEELING, DISFIGURED
IN UNIMAGINABLE WAYS. BLACK BLOOD SPILLING OUT OF HIS MOUTH.

WITHOUT THINKING, NATHAN SWINGS THE MACHETE, PINS THE
ZOMBIE'S ARM AGAINST THE WALL -- POP, POP, POP -- THREE MORE
ROUNDS EJECT INTO THE WALL, EMPTYING THE CHAMBER.

HARPER PICKS UP THE SLEDGE, SWINGS IT INTO THE ZOMBIE'S BACK.
WE HEAR THE DRY SNAP OF BROKEN RIBS.

THE ZOMBIE FALLS TO THE FLOOR.

Harper climbs up the LADDER. Nathan follows closely behind.

EXT. HAUNTED HOUSE, HATCH - NIGHT

Harper pulls herself through the hatch, onto the roof.
Morning fog lingers. The sun about to rise.

Nathan reaches up for a hand but --

THE HATCH IS SUDDENLY KICKED CLOSED!

THE METAL DOOR SLAMS HARD ON NATHAN'S HANDS, CRUSHING HIS
FINGERS, TRAPPING HIM INSIDE.

Harper turns to see the WITCH.

INT. HIDDEN PASSAGE, HATCH - NIGHT

Nathan dangles over the ladder in agony, unable to get his hands free.

                    NATHAN
          OPEN THE DOOR! OPEN THE DOOR!

EXT. HAUNTED HOUSE, HATCH - NIGHT

Nathan's cries are MUFFLED outside.

Harper takes a swing with the SLEDGEHAMMER but misses, the momentum carrying her down the sloped rooftop.

INT. HIDDEN PASSAGE, HATCH - NIGHT

The ZOMBIE starts to stir, slowly coming to.

EXT. HAUNTED HOUSE, HATCH - NIGHT

Harper winds up again. Doing her best to fight back, but she's no warrior. Swings and misses.

The WITCH closes in and Harper JUST STRAIGHT UP THROWS THE SLEDGEHAMMER. IT AWKWARDLY CATCHES THE WITCH'S LEG, TRIPPING HER.

Harper opens the HATCH. Nathan's fingers are released and he drops below --

The ZOMBIE begins to rise.

The WITCH grabs Harper from behind, but Harper is able to wrestle her under the hatch door.

Nathan climbs back up the ladder with his BROKEN FINGERS, in excruciating pain. He strangles the WITCH from below and --

HARPER SLAMS THE HATCH DOOR ON THE WITCH'S FACE:

ONCE

TWICE

THREE TIMES

EACH BLOW REMOVING A PIECE OF HER MASK, UNTIL WE SEE A **HAUNTING PALE COMPLEXION. WRINKLED SKIN. FADED LIKE LEATHER. MAYBE IT IS LEATHER? SEWN INTO THE EPIDERMIS.**

<u>**WITH BLACK MOLES SURGICALLY ADDED OR GROWN, MANIFESTING LIKE OPEN WOUNDS. CATARACTS IN BOTH EYES. 1950s STYLE SILVER HAIR PINNED BACK IN A BUN.**</u>

Nathan pulls the WITCH down through the hatch, then joins Harper on the roof.

They make a run for the parking lot.

INT. MAZE < MIRROR ROOM - NIGHT

The CLOWN stops in the MIRROR MAZE. Catches his breath.

INT. MAZE < LEFT PASSAGE - NIGHT

Finally, after a moment, he exits into the passage, examines the BLACK OILY WALLS that surround him.

EXT. HAUNTED HOUSE, PARKING LOT - NIGHT

Harper and Nathan race across the parking lot. They are instantly reminded of the barbed wire PERIMETER FENCE trapping them inside.

But that doesn't stop them. <u>They didn't come this far only to come this far</u>.

They arrive at Evan's car. Driver-side door open. Windows broken. Someone's clearly already searched for keys, but Nathan does a quick look anyway.

Harper hears something.

                    HARPER
                (hushed)
            Nathan, look.

Outside the haunted house, a couple FIGURES emerge in the distance.

                    HARPER
                (hushed)
            Let's go.

They start running towards the perimeter fence, but Nathan skids to a stop.

                    NATHAN
            I'm right behind you.

Nathan runs back to Evan's car and pops the trunk. Inside the trunk, he finds --

                    HIS LUCKY BASEBALL BAT

-- the one he hit the 500 footer over the right field wall, securing a school record.

Nathan takes the BAT and a COTTON BLANKET.

The ZOMBIE notices the commotion and signals the others.

INT. MAZE < LEFT PASSAGE - NIGHT

Inside the LEFT PASSAGE, the CLOWN lights a MATCH.

He raises the match to the BLACK WALLS.

THE WALLS CATCH FIRE INSTANTLY. THE FLAMES SPREAD THROUGHOUT THE ROOM. SOON EXPANDING TO THE ENTIRE HAUNTED HOUSE.

THIS IS WHY THE WALLS WERE COVERED IN OIL AND NOT PAINT. THEY WERE ALWAYS PLANNING ON BURNING THIS PLACE TO THE GROUND.

EXT. HAUNTED HOUSE, PERIMETER FENCE - NIGHT

Harper climbs the fence. One leg at a time. As fast as she can muster.

Nathan's not far behind. He tosses the BLANKET up over the BARBED WIRE. It creates a safe barrier to cross over.

Harper goes first. Even with the blanket, it is brutal and challenging. Cutting up her arms and legs. This is what it's like to actually climb through a barbed wire fence.

The ZOMBIE approaches. Reloads and raises the .38 S&W.

NATHAN TURNS. BLINKS. HE KNOWS WHAT HE HAS TO DO.

NATHAN RUNS HEAD FIRST INTO THE MOST DANGEROUS SITUATION OF HIS LIFE.

POP POP POP -- NATHAN TAKES TWO BULLETS IN THE TORSO. BUT IT DOESN'T STOP HIM. HE JUST KEEPS RUNNING INTO THE PITCH. FEARLESS.

NATHAN'S HANDS TIGHTEN AROUND THE BAT -- A FAMILIAR FEELING -- FEELS LIKE DESTINY -- AS HE WINDS UP -- WITH STAGGERING SPEED AND STRENGTH -- AND *WHOOSH* -- THE BAT SLICES THROUGH THE AIR AND CONNECTS WITH THE ZOMBIE'S HAND -- SENDING THE .38 FLYING INTO THE DISTANCE.

THE ZOMBIE BUCKLES -- ALL HE SEES IS A BLUR OF WOOD -- AS THE BAT CRASHES INTO HIS SKULL.

Harper gets stuck. Doesn't think she can keep going. A dark inferno grows in the background, engulfing the haunted house.

> NATHAN
> I got you.

Nathan arrives at the top of the fence and helps Harper over safely.

But her foot snags the BLANKET and rips down with her to the other side. Harper lands painfully below.

Nathan tries to cross the RAW WIRE, but without the blanket, it cuts him to shreds; capturing him in its deadly serrated grip. He violently tries to work himself free but it just makes things worse.

> NATHAN
> Run Harper!

Harper starts to run away, but stops.

No, fuck that. She's not going to be a trope or a cliche. She's not going to be a final girl.

Harper climbs back up the fence and grabs Nathan's hand. They share a moment, albeit brief.

> HARPER
> I got you too.

EXT. FOREST - NIGHT

Harper runs through the forest, supporting Nathan who can barely walk. She's covered in blood and tears.

Branches and leaves whip by. She puts her hand out to protect Nathan's face and eyes.

A tree catches Harper's arm. She almost falls but keeps running.

EXT. FOREST ROAD - NIGHT

She stumbles into a clearing, out of breath and panting. There's an empty highway road.

Empty except for SAM'S RED PICKUP TRUCK waiting in the distance.

Relief washes over Harper's face. They're saved.

EXT. HIGHWAY ROAD - SUNRISE

Harper races down an empty highway.

EXT. CAMPUS - MORNING

Harper takes a hard left. Speeds through the campus. Passes
the School of Law. Morris Library. Saluki Stadium.

Harper notices Red & Blue lights ahead...

COP CARS AND AMBULANCES BLOW BY IN THE OPPOSITE DIRECTION.

Harper doesn't look back. Just keeps driving. Until...

INT. HOSPITAL, LOBBY - MORNING

Harper carries Nathan into a hospital lobby. They are swarmed
by alarmed medical STAFF and EMTs. Nathan is carried
immediately to ER. He hands something to Harper...

IT'S THE MOONSTONE RING.

She stares at her mother's ring in disbelief. The staff tries
to wrestle Harper onto a stretcher, but she breaks away.

She slides the ring onto her finger. There's one last thing
she needs to do...

EXT. SUBURBAN HOME - MORNING

The pick-up truck finally arrives at a quiet SUBURBAN HOME.
We've seen this place somewhere before...

WHITE PICKET FENCE. AMERICAN FLAG ON THE PORCH. THIS IS
HARPER'S CHILDHOOD HOME.

Harper steps out of the truck. She nervously approaches the
porch. Reaches her arm out. Knocks three times.

A light turns on inside. Harper takes a deep breath.
Terrified of what comes next.

The front door slowly opens and...

HARPER AND HER **MOTHER** REGARD EACH OTHER FOR THE FIRST TIME IN
YEARS.

THEY MOVE IN FOR A LONG EMBRACE AS --

THE CLOWN EMERGES FROM BEHIND HARPER'S MOM!!!!

SLAM TO:

INT. HOSPITAL, ROOM - DAY

Harper snaps awake. She's covered in sweat. Doesn't know
where she is.

She takes stock of her surroundings. A small hospital room.
She's hooked up to an EKG. Two OFFICERS stand guard outside.

She catches her breath. Thank god it was just a dream...

She sits upright in the hospital bed. The blood on her face
has been mostly cleaned, but the bruise under her eye is
clearly visible. Her exposed shoulder has stitches from the
shrapnel wound. Her hands are bandaged.

She notices the MOONSTONE RING on the tray. Picks it up and
puts it on her finger. Takes a deep breath. It was just a
dream. Everything is gonna be okay.

A NURSE enters the room.

                    NURSE
          Sorry to wake you, Sweetheart.
               (beat)
          Just need your signature on a
          couple release forms.

Harper blinks. Oh no...

CUT TO:

INT. WHITE PANEL VAN - SUNSET

CLOSE ON a stack of Haunt release forms. We see Harper's
mom's address is listed under "Emergency Contact" on the form
she filled out.

Next to the forms there's a plastic vacuform CLOWN mask.
Gloved hands turn the wheel. Out the dash we see a quiet
residential neighborhood.

EXT. SUBURBAN HOME - SUNSET

The white panel van slows to a stop.

The Clown, now wearing the vacuform mask, approaches the suburban home. He's holding his SLEDGEHAMMER.

INT. SUBURBAN HOME - SUNSET

The security chain snaps in two as the front door is forced open. The Clown steps inside.

The living room is shrouded in dark shadows. Harper stands alone ten feet away. She looks startled. Terrified even.

The Clown gazes at her with soulless black eyes. They both know he's here to finish the job.

The Clown takes a step forward...

Wait something's wrong.

He looks down at his boot...

His feet are stuck in ADHESIVE. That's weird.

Just then a familiar melody starts to play through the house...

The Clown looks up to Harper, but she's no longer there. A BLUETOOTH SPEAKER is on the table playing POP GOES THE WEASEL.

He starts to panic. He pulls at his boot. Forcing it off the adhesive.

He gets one foot free. Starts working on the other foot.

The sole of his boot rips off and he tumbles forward.

He reaches his arms out to catch himself and his hand lands on a... BED OF NAILS!

Harper has turned her house into a haunt.

The Clown screams in pain.

THE MUSIC SLOWS TO A STOP.

...

THE CLOWN RIPS HIS HAND OFF THE NAILS. HE HEARS SOMETHING AROUND THE CORNER.

. . .

HE GLANCES AROUND. SEARCHING THE SHADOWS. EYES LAND ON AN
<u>EMPTY GUN RACK</u> ABOVE THE FIREPLACE.

. . .

AS HARPER ENTERS FRAME. GUN RAISED. HER FACE SOFTENS AS SHE
SQUEEZES THE TRIGGER --

                    HARPER
          Let's take off your mask.

                                        SLAM TO BLACK.

UNMASKED

Interview by Scott Myers

Screenwriter/Professor Scott Myers met with Bryan Woods & Scott Beck on October 12, 2021 for the following interview.

Scott Myers: *How did two affable, nice young fellows from Iowa develop such a keen interest in writing and directing horror movies which scare the hell out of audiences?*

Scott Beck: I think we absolutely adore movies that provoke, and stories that explore the darker side of humanity. It might be because we grew up in Iowa in a very safe and stable neighborhood and environment, so we are able to invite the worst situations possible into our lives.

I just remember the movies I watched when I was way too young, like *Alien*, or *Robocop*, or Cronenberg's *The Fly*. I saw those when I was five or six years old and those are movies that really scar you. From, first and foremost, just a visceral standpoint, but as I got slightly older, like 15, I saw those from a character standpoint. Something like *The Fly*, how there's a transformative process that overtakes a character emotionally in addition to physically and the combination of those two elements in a genre movie were really terrifying but really beautiful in terms of the execution on film.

SM: *Bryan, were you exposed to these movies when you were that young?*

Bryan Woods: Yeah, my parents were very cool about taking me to R-rated movies. It was not uncommon in our household. I remember seeing *Terminator 2* when I was in first grade and loving it and just loving movies in general. My mom would always rent the *Alien* movies for me, and Scott and I, I don't know, maybe we were a little braver than most kids, but we've always loved genre, and we've always loved how that rollercoaster ride is so thrilling in those movies and it really did affect us from a young age.

SM: *So, like Tarantino's mom was taking him to these R-rated movies when he was six and seven years old. Again, all you bad parents out there, good for you. You're creating cinema masters.*

But let's talk about chronology here. So you write the spec script A Quiet Place. That gets set up at Paramount, ironically with the person who makes the noisiest movies of all time, Michael Bay. That gets produced and goes on to gross over 300 million dollars in worldwide box office ticket sales. Where did Haunt slot into this timeline with the journey of A Quiet Place from spec to feature?

BW: We actually wrote them at the same time. *Haunt* was something that Broken Road, our producers on the project, brought to us. They were noodling on a few ideas and one of the things they said was, "well, we're interested in doing a movie where a group of kids go to a haunted house and the scares they encounter turn out to be real." They didn't have much more than that. And that didn't really spark our interest. We weren't like, "oh wow, we have to tell that story." We just said, "okay, interesting. What do you want to do with it?" And they kept saying, "you guys do whatever you want with it!"

We were really resistant at first. The whole time, it was a series of us trying to convince ourselves, "do we have an idea that would be compelling? And if we're going to do a Halloween movie, then what's Halloween really about?" To us, Halloween is about dress-up and make-believe, putting on a mask and being somebody that you're not for an evening. We started to filter the concept through this theme of "masks" and thought, maybe we can tell a story about a young woman who is putting on a metaphorical mask. She's trying to pretend that everything is okay in her life and everything is fine. But she's in this abusive relationship and everything is *not* fine. As we started to get excited about some of the ideas we were circling on *Haunt*, our producers commissioned us to write the script. We were actually able to write both *A Quiet Place* and *Haunt* simultaneously, and it was really fun for us to hop back and forth between two projects that we felt were completely different.

With *A Quiet Place*, which in our minds was this "elevated" horror piece about family and very character-driven, and then the other side of our sensibilities said "that's so pretentious to think of horror as an 'elevated' genre. Haunt is going to be this thrill machine. It's going be an exercise in thrills and scares and fun. A bit of a throwback to John Carpenter." So, we were jumping back and forth. One week Scott would work on *A Quiet Place*, I'd work on *Haunt*, and then we'd trade scripts, and then Scott would work on *Haunt* and I'd work on *A Quiet Place*. It was really fun to jump between those two different sides of the genre.

SM: *They really are similar but different, aren't they?*

SB: Yeah, the clear Venn diagram in retrospect for us – and I think this is partly about the writing process – is with both projects we have the high concept, but until we know metaphorically, or emotionally, or thematically what the drive of the story really is, we're at a standstill. It's the same thing with *A Quiet Place* where we were living with that concept for years and years, but until we discovered that this is about a family on a farm that has suffered a great loss, and they'd be broken and not able to metaphorically communicate even if these aliens had never invaded. Once we clicked on that with *A Quiet Place*, we were off to the races. The same thing with *Haunt*, as Bryan said, once we figured out the idea that metaphorically everybody's wearing a mask in real life, that was the entry point for us to really start getting into script pages.

SM: *Let's talk about the logline of your movie Haunt. "On Halloween, a group of friends encounter an extreme haunted house that promises to feed on their darkest fears, The night turns deadly as they come to the horrifying realization that some nightmares are real."*

Now personally, I make it a habit to not go into haunted houses, whether they are extreme or otherwise, but is this something you've done in the past or researched?

SB: Absolutely. I mean, our childhood growing up in Iowa every October was going to haunted houses that were really lo-fi. Meaning there would be local groups of horror aficionados that would rent a cornfield and put up a terrifying maze or convert an old factory that had been closed for 50 years and just build whatever they could build within a three-week timespan and with a thousand dollars and just throw that into the vibe and the feeling of going into the unknown. That to us was the aesthetic and touchstone for writing the script and bringing it to life as directors. We didn't want the haunted house to feel like Universal Studios' Halloween Horror Nights where everything is very produced and as soon you turn a corner something's going to jump out at you. We like to have restraint and have characters go down the hallways and nothing would happen, and the absence of a scare would create suspense. Or other times when a villain comes out, you think they're going to be threatening but they're actually there to help. And because they're wearing a mask, you don't know whether or not you can trust them. You never know what's behind that mask.

SM: *Horror seems to me the one genre where they play around with tropes the most. Here you've got a classic example of a trope: a group of young people gets into trouble. You even acknowledge in the script for Haunt: "Evan 22, nerdy shapeless try-hard who is a bit confrontational. The last of our group." So what are your thoughts about using, inverting, and otherwise dealing with tropes in the horror genre?*

BW: I love everything you're saying because the genre has familiar goal posts that are fun to hit and lean into at times to make the audience feel comfortable, and make them feel like they're in a place where they've been before and then, in turn, use that to surprise them. The big breakthrough for us during the writing of this movie was letting the villains run the show. We wanted to set the table with as many conventions as we could come up with, which is fun as writers when creating a group of characters. There's the jock and there's the disapproving best friend, whatever the clichés are… we set the table with these familiar elements and we move those conventional characters into this haunted house, and the fun part for us was letting the villains run amok and do whatever they want to do. A big part of our process is outlining the movie – not in granular detail – we like leaving enough room and air in the script to let things happen that we don't expect. So once these familiar characters were inside the haunted house – inside this familiar premise – then the villains started doing whatever they wanted, things that we didn't expect.

A perfect example is the ghost character of Mitch. We were writing a sequence where we knew Nathan would be in this corridor surrounded by sheet-covered bodies, and the ghost character was going to close in on him and the expected version – and what our outline said – is, "the ghost character attacks Nathan." But the ghost character, as we're writing the scene, didn't *want* to attack Nathan. The ghost character wanted to turn the lights on and approach Nathan and say, "Hey man, everything's okay. Are you alright? How can I help?" And all of the sudden the ghost sounds like this normal person, so little things like that, like letting the villains dictate the story and bring us away from convention and do things differently, is fun for us. It's one of our favorite things to do as writers.

SB: That also led us to explore the behind the scenes of the haunt too. We started being like, "Okay, we can actually see the villains' break room," and you start seeing the normalcy of how they're putting this haunt together, and they're not these super villains. In fact, their plans start getting tripped up as the night goes along, and that became interesting to us because it starts grounding the story and hopefully subverting some of the conventions that you otherwise would expect. The villains make mistakes and stupid decisions sometimes, like real people.

I think that extends to the set pieces too. Scott [Myers], you had mentioned about one of the scenes feeling inspired by *Roman Holiday* where [Audrey Hepburn and Gregory Peck] stick their hand into a hole and you don't know what's going to happen. And that's one of those scenes where when a character sticks their hand in a hole in a horror movie, the audience knows something bad is going to happen. That's a convention. That's a clear expectation. What we had the control over was, when does that scare land? And those decisions help turn it into suspense versus it just being a jump scare, and so a lot of scenes like that were about Bryan and I going back and forth in a writing phase saying, okay, we have our characters put their hand in the hole, and then they take it out and then they have to put it in again – so at what point does the audience expect something bad to happen? And then let's not just go one step beyond their expectations. Let's go two or three steps beyond until the audience lets their guard down, so that when the scare does happen, it hopefully has a bigger impact. So that's indicative of the script as a whole, where we're trying to take what the audience expects and then try to go beyond that, where we feel like we have the license to.

SM: *That to me was what I thought was kind of genius about the concept. You get this group of young people in this extreme haunted house and it lends itself to the greatest hits of cinematic homages. You got a couple tunnel scenes. And of course, I'm claustrophobic, so it's like Alien, where Dallas gets attacked. Or Nathan hiding in the curtain in the break room, and I'm thinking we're in the closet scene in Halloween or Blue Velvet. Or the backward writing on the wall feels like The Shining. So how many of those things were intentional? How many of those things were just serendipitous?*

BW: Well, we're movie lovers, so we can't ignore our influences and we're always studying those films. I can't say that *Blue Velvet*, the closet scene, was a conscious inspiration, it's not something Scott and I ever talked about. But that's a masterful scene. And a big part of our job is watching our heroes' work and reading our favorite scripts, reading the work of our favorite writers, and just remembering and loving how they do it and studying how they do it. That's the fun for us and, yeah, it always finds its way into our work if we're lucky.

SM: *So, I have this image of you two... "Okay, Okay, Bryan, Scott, we gotta crack this thing, we gotta come up with those set pieces," you know, drinking old stale beer, eating a pizza and just brainstorming. How did you come up with all these set pieces? Because it's like one crazy thing after another. What was the process like?*

SB: It was really drawing upon the haunted houses of our childhood, knowing that all of them had this raw, understated quality when you walk in, but the design would amplify and get scarier. And there would be the rotating vortex tunnels, rooms that had silly mirrors. And then thinking, from a writing perspective, what if somebody was actually behind those mirrors? And trying to elevate each room idea one step further.

But we were also thinking about extreme haunted houses, where you hand over your own vulnerabilities, you sign waivers, and part of that gimmick could be a charade to make it feel more intense than it is, but there's also that question in your mind like, "what if this actually is real?" And so I think any time that we could draw back on things that felt grounded to us or you can point to in reality, the better, because we wanted these characters and situations to feel like they were cut from real life.

SM: *The current state of Hollywood and TV is awash with nostalgia. You mentioned John Carpenter as a touch point, and when I watched Haunt I was thinking, there's Funhouse, House, Slumber Party Massacre, you know, some of those movies from the 80s. Were you trying to say we're going to do an homage, or get into the spirit of those movies from the 80s and 90s? Or what were some of the movies that inspired you?*

BW: We were trying to do something specific, which is be nostalgic and modern at the same time. That's kind of a weird thing to say, but it's like we were standing on the shoulders of Tobe Hooper's *Funhouse* and even *Texas Chainsaw Massacre* to a certain extent, and certainly John Carpenter films like *Halloween*. There are many influences that are obvious that we're standing on, but we didn't want the movie to feel retro. It wasn't like we wanted the throwback synth score and the grainy 16-millimeter look of those movies. We wanted it to feel like now. And to a certain extent, the movie's also, maybe not consciously, but certainly subconsciously, it's almost nostalgic for the 90s slasher genre in a weird way too, which is odd to say because it's not something we talk about intellectually. We're not like, "Oh man, remember the slashers of the 90s," but it's what we grew up with.

That's what we were watching when we were kids, and so we can't really escape that.

SB: But also from the 90s, David Fincher's *The Game* was a movie we were thinking of outside the horror genre, just from the standpoint of always keeping the audience on their toes and not knowing left from right and who's actually telling the truth and who's not, because we thought, especially from the villain standpoint, the disorientation can be more suspenseful than a villain just running around with a weapon. It's the distrust or having to have the trust in another character to hopefully lead you out of danger, only to find out, no, they actually were maybe the most dangerous of all.

SM: *It's an ensemble piece, which I think is pretty typical for these kind of movies, but there is a lead protagonist, and that's this young woman named Harper. She's in an abusive relationship, and when we first meet her, she's covering up this wound. That seems like that unlocked something for you. Is that fair to say?*

SB: Absolutely. We always try to look at incidents from either our own life or the life of loved ones or close friends, and that unlocks a reality that makes us more adept at fleshing out a story, fleshing out a character, fleshing out an emotional journey. And so, when we only had the concept, that wasn't enough for us to get inspired and feel like we had a direction. But once Bryan and I had enough conversations about the metaphor, that everybody's wearing a mask, we determine how that folds into a character type. And then as we did with *A Quiet Place* and same with any scripts we write, Bryan and I draw upon people that we know in our own circle. Of course we never want to put 100% of who they are on screen, just to be respective of privacy, but that shorthand becomes a big part of it. We have a shared history because Bryan and I have known each other since we were 11 years old, so we grew up with the same people. We've known each other's family for so long. And so there's a kinship that we have; a closeness that we're able to share stories and then inject those wherever possible into our scripts, whether it's the character of Harper or the character of Nathan or any of the other characters that hopefully gives them dimensionality.

SM: *So let's talk about the script, because you've got this script for* Haunt *being published, and you're carving out your own little niche in Hollywood, because you got the stylistic thing where you broke all of these supposed rules with* A Quiet Place. *And my take is that you really wanted to do whatever you could to make the story pop on the page, and we see the same style here in* Haunt. *Especially in terms of scene description, capitalization, underlining, italics, bold, altering font types and size. So could you talk about that approach to screenplay style and philosophy of saying, "screw the rules, we're just going to do what we need to do in order to make this thing work"?*

BW: We've been writing scripts and reading scripts since we were kids, and the rules are always such a big conversation when you're 13 and you're surfing the internet wondering how do you write a script, and what are the rules of formatting. In some circles these are very rigid things, and in many ways, screenplays have looked the same since *The Wizard of Oz*. Screenplays haven't changed that much. And maybe they shouldn't. On one hand, they are kind of a technical document, but on another hand, they are sales tools, and you are writing the dream of the movie on the page, and you want everyone who reads that script to see the trailer in their head and to lean in and get invested. And so, where we can, when it's not too obnoxious, we use every tool in our tool box as writers to get people to feel the experience of the movie. In the case of *A Quiet Place*, the movie had hardly any dialogue, and we really wanted to sell this silent film experience, and so that required some snazzy formatting and the use of images in the script, and we were writing *Haunt* at the same time and thinking a lot about format, ruminating on it and thinking about where we could bend the rules and not bend the rules.

In the case of *Haunt*, there's a moment in the script where the characters branch off into two different directions in this maze and we thought, let's throw the slug of the right passage of the maze onto the right margin, and let's throw the slug for the left passage onto the left margin, and it's just this little visual thing that you barely notice. Now does it help the read? Yeah, maybe. Maybe it orients you or maybe it's just fun, maybe we're just having fun writing and that's also okay. We don't mind giving ourselves that license. And with the villains, we would give them this cute little innocent colored text. Like the Clown had this rainbow text, and the Witch had green text, and the Devil had red text. Signifiers for the color of their masks. And in our heads, we're making them less threatening. We're making them cute on the page. It almost looks silly and that's exactly in our minds what their masks are going to look like in the finished film. They're going to look a little benign, they're going look a little retro and safe. And when those masks come off, the formatting gets really gnarly, and we get into underlining and bolding, and italicized fonts because what's under the mask is so scary. We're always thinking about these weird formatting elements. And it's just fun.

SM: *Yeah, you indulge in it also with what I call "psychological writing", where you're commenting in scene description. Like there's a narrator making a comment, or you're dipping inside a character's inner life. For example, "this is a mask Harper regularly wears. A look that says everything's okay. You wouldn't even know she's been through the worst week of her life," or, "Bailey gives Nathan an overly affectionate hug that makes him a little uncomfortable. They have an on again/off again dynamic. Nathan can never really tell when Bailey's into him," or, "Now Bailey's riding Ty. See, that's what we're talking about." Now you're really getting conversational with the reader, "that's what we are talking about. Is Bailey into Nathan? Playing games? Who knows." Let's talk about that psychological writing. You want the reader to feel something, you want to have an emotional experience when you read a script.*

SB: I think it comes from a standpoint that scripts can be blueprints for movies and you can read a script just as a technical document. For us, we also appreciate when scripts can stand alone just as a piece of writing that's engaging and interesting, and I think *Haunt* hopefully hits that mark, but also works as a document in service of bringing the movie to the screen with our collaborators. So, as directors, we want to make sure the script is communicating the intent that may be fed into an actor's interpretation of the scene. So for the scene when Nathan feels uncomfortable about the way Bailey's acting around him – if we're able to have a short hand in the script with a chunk of description, then the actor has something to latch onto from the very first moment that they read the script, that's great, because that helps the emotional journey start to develop in their minds in a way that hopefully coalesces into a fully fleshed out character once we're on set. But I think like Bryan said, sometimes it's just fun to be living in the moment when writing the pages, you try to communicate what you're feeling through the lens of the character and you just put that down on paper. Sometimes we need to go back and edit ourselves during rewrites because we might go too deep into that type of description, but other times we just give ourselves the license to stretch beyond what the rules of screenwriting are and just enjoy the process on the page and try to tell a story. That's the most fundamental rule.

SM: *That right there, I'm going to print out, because I tell my students all the time that during the first draft, just have fun. Just go for it. You can always scale things back. At least just give yourself over to the story and the characters.*

So Haunt currently has a 100% audience rating on Rotten Tomatoes. It's like this cult movie. What's that make you feel? What's been the response to this movie?

BW: We're really surprised by how it's found an audience. It's actually been one of the most gratifying things in our career because the movie came together with such humble means. It was kind of a smaller indie film, and really with this project, we were thinking about the audience the whole time. That was our North Star. We were thinking about it as, what's the ride of the movie and what's a fun thrill machine that you would go see on a Friday night, or that you would rent on VHS at Blockbuster and tell your friends about, and make them watch. And we're so grateful that people are finding it.

SM: *You mentioned this thrill machine, so I encourage people to read the script and fortunately they're going to be able to do that and experience the thrill machine in the written form, because you're publishing this. Could you talk a little bit about that?*

BW: I'm glad you asked because we have a deep nostalgia for the whole concept of the "published screenplay". When Scott and I were growing up in Iowa as young filmmakers, there was nothing more exciting than going to the local bookstore and perusing the aisles and seeing all of these scripts they used to publish all the time. It was such a common thing. We'd buy the script for Paul Thomas Anderson's *Magnolia* and read, "Wow, this is what a script looks like," and thumb through the pages and hold it in our hands and read the Q&A afterwards at the end of the book. It's something that we've just always loved. We collect scripts, and any time a writer puts one out, we snap it up because it's just something that we love as fans. That's all to say that selfishly we're hoping this book encourages more screenwriters to put their work out there so we have more screenplays to collect.

Scott Myers has written 30 projects at nearly every major Hollywood studio and broadcast network. He hosts GoIntoTheStory.com, which Writers' Digest named "Best of the Best Scriptwriting Website." He is the author of the book *The Protagonist's Journey: An Introduction to Character-Driven Screenwriting and Storytelling.* An assistant professor at DePaul University, Scott is a graduate of the University of Virginia and Yale University Divinity School.

CAST & CREW

SIERRA PICTURES Presents

A

BROKEN ROAD / NICKEL CITY PICTURES
Production

HAUNT

Written and Directed by
SCOTT BECK & BRYAN WOODS

Produced by
TODD GARNER
MARK FASANO
VISHAL RUNGTA
ANKUR RUNGTA
ELI ROTH

Executive Producers
NICK MEYER
MARC SCHABERG
JOSIE LIANG
JON WAGNER
TOBIAS WEYMAR
SEAN ROBINS
JEREMY STEIN

Director of Photography
RYAN SAMUL

Production Designer
AUSTIN GORG

Edited by
TEREL GIBSON

Costume Designer
NANCY COLLINI

Music by
tomandandy

Casting by
NANCY NAYOR, C.S.A

CAST

Harper	Katie Stevens
Nathan	Will Brittain
Bailey	Lauryn McClain
Evan	Andrew Caldwell
Angela	Shazi Raja
Mallory	Schuyler Helford
Ty	Phillip Johnson-Richardson
Ghost	Chaney Morrow
Clown	Justin Marxen
Witch	Terri Partyka
Vampire	Justin Rose
Devil	Damian Maffei
Zombie	Schuyler White
Sam	Samuel Hunt
Young Woman	Karra Robinson
DJ Poltergeis	Brent Geisler
Nurse	Karli Hall
Young Harper	Briana Tedesco
Harper's Mom	Katy Arnold
Harper's Dad	William Arnold
Voice of Witch	Lynnanne Zager
Stunt Coordinator	T.J. White
Stunt Riggers	Ele Bardha
	Corrina Roshea
	Tony Lanesky
Stunt Doubles (Ms. Stevens)	Nicole Marines
	Heather Long
Stunt Double (Ms. McClain)	April Sutton

Stunt Double (Ms. Raja)	Shai DeBroux
Stunt Double (Ms. Partyka)	Jessi Fisher
Stunt Doubles (Mr. Maffei)	Remington Steele
	Jason Cekanski

Unit Production Manager
JON D. WAGNER

First Assistant Director
DOUG TURNER

Second Assistant Director
TAMI KUMIN

CREW

Art Director	Jason Perrine
Set Decorator	Kay Wolfley
Camera Operator	Alexander Elkins
First Assistant Photographers	Jefri Meintjes
	Geoffrey Storts
Second Assistant	Megan Cafferty
Photographers	
	Joe Bou
Steadicam Operator	Dave Schwandner
"B" Camera Operators	Nikk Hern-Sutton, SOC
	Kameron Mogadam
"B" First Assistant	Michael Wooten
Photographer	
"B" Second Assistant	Jeremy M. Borg
Photographers	
	Anthony Pesce
Digital Imaging Technician	Matt Mulcahey
Script Supervisor	Kelsey Forren
Sound Mixer	Chris Polczinski
Boom Operators	Tasha Ladwig
	Brandon Cooper

Chief Lighting Technician	Andrew Hubbard
Assistant Chief Lighting Technician	Lucas James Ankney
Chief Rigging Electrician	Chance Madison
Assistant Chief Rigging Electrician	Joey Morrissey
Electricians	Randy Miller
	Thomas William Vincent
	T.S. Green
	Jake Knueven
	Aaron Arnett
	Jacob Lyon
	Kyle Schuler
First Company Grip	Jeff Fisher
Second Company Grip	John Zanardelli
First Company Rigging Grip	Zachary Cahill
Second Company Rigging Grip	Dean A. Ross
Dolly Grip Operator	Mike Dittiacur
Grips	Tori Roloson
	Matthew Legner
	Aria Brice
	Charles Glassman
	Jennifer Puckett
Rigging Grips	Rasheen Crawley
	Clifton Radford
	Michael James
Supervising Sound Editor	Mac Smith
Special Effects Provided by	Tolin FX
Special Effects Coordinator	Steve Tolin
Key Special Effects Technician	Raymond M. Tasillo
Special Effects Technicians	Nicholas Barrington
	Chris Thamann
Location Manager	Alan Forbes
Assistant Location Managers	Jennifer Combs
	Nick Pirrmann
Property Master	Steve Ochoa

Assistant Property Master	Shelby Hamet
Lead Person	Brett Jackson
Set Dressing Foreperson	Brian Bergen
Set Dressers	Michael Reuter
	Christopher Wald
On Set Dresser	Claire Gryce
Set Decoration Buyer	Samantha Drake
Costume Supervisor	Robin Fields
Key Costumer	Jaclyn Laravie
Costumers	Elizabeth Galbraith
	Mary Murphy
Textile Artist	Kathleen Akaka
Makeup Department Head	Jodi Byrne
Key Makeup Artist	Jason Ervin
Makeup Artists	Amber Johnson
	Anna Richardson
Makeup Effects Artists	Hugo Villaseñor
	Chris Bridges
Hair Department Head	Scott H. Reeder
Key Hairstylist	Rachel Bayer
Hairstylists	Velia Asimus
	Lindsey Howard
	Samanatha Maloney
Production Supervisor	Brianna Fischer
Production Coordinator	Annie Mahoney
Production Secretary	Claire Jago
Second Second Assistant	Casey Shelton
Director	
Art Department Coordinator	Natalie LeCompte
Art Department Production	Ashley Thomas
Assistant	
Casting Associate	Andrew Henry
Local Casting	D. Lynn Meyers, C.S.A.
Still Photographers	Brian Douglas
	Richard Baker
Production Accountant	Sue McGraw
First Assistant Accountant	Debra Kaufman

Second Assistant Accountant	Chelsea McGraw
Post Production Supervisors	John Portnoy
	Renee Minasian
Assistant Editors	Kathryn Prescott
	Alex de la Peña
	John Paul Ungaretti
Additional Editor	Robert Mead
Post Production Sound	Skywalker Sound
Services Provided by	A Lucasfilm Ltd. Company
	Marin County, California
Re-Recording Mixers	Tony Villaflor
	Brandon Proctor
Dialogue Editor	Chris Gridley
Foley Editor	Luke Dunn Gielmuda
Music Editor	Richard Gould
Foley Artist	Shelley Roden
Foley Mixer	Scott Curtis
Engineering Services	Jim Austin
Digital Editorial Support	David Peifer
Post Production Sound	Cathy Shirk
Accountant	
Post Production Finance	Mike Peters
Manager	
Client Services	Eva Porter
Scheduling	Carrie Perry
Head of Engineering	Steve Morris
Head of Production	Jon Null
General Manager	Josh Lowden
Assistant Composer	Eric Jourgensen
Score Production Consultant	Scott Williams
Score Recorded at	tomandandy Studidos
ADR Recordists	Colin Rogers
	Travis Mackay
	Sébastien Rochon

ADR Voice Casting	Chris White
	Greg Crawford
	Mike Rivera
	Corey Norman
	Fabiana Arrastia
	Susan Boyajian
Construction Coordinator	Josh Lamping
Standby Painters	Jennifer Acus-Smith
	Brent Wachter
Standby Carpenters	Tim Brown
	Daniel Fullenkamp
	Thomas S. Gardner
	Deeann Shane
	Michael C. Waechter
Scenic Artist	Melissa Bennett
Props Maker	Gabby Leithsceal
Production Assistants	Jake Heineke
	Ashley Collinsworth
	Victoria McDevitt
	Stephen Koller
	Cathy Holt
	Robena Teneralli
	John Megliorino
	Jeff Seemann
	Zachary Waldridge
Transportation Captain	Jeff Montgomery
Drivers	William Lloyd
	Brandon Leach
	Ralph Metzger
	James Downton
	Mike Lilly
Medics	Karen Burke
	Nelson Livingston
	Tocarra Welch
Craft Service	Kyle Costello
Catering by	Firestone Catering

FOR SIERRA PICTURES

President, International Sales and Distribution	Jonathan Kier
Executive Vice President, International Marketing and Publicity	Joey Monteiro
Senior Vice President, International Sales	Jenia Gorton
Senior Vice President, Legal and Business Affairs	Kendra Dousette
Senior Vice President, International Operations and Administration	Cynthia Griffiths
Vice President, International Sales and Distribution	Nick Sherry
Vice President, Publicity	Antonia Gray
Manager, Distribution	Lissette Jean-Marie
Coordinator, Marketing and Publicity	Nida Karnani
Manager, International Sales and Distribution	Fiodor Otero
Creative Executive	Laurel Thompson
Coordinator, Acquisitions and Productions	Janice Lee
Senior Vice President, Distribution Services and Operations	Scarlett Pettyjohn
Senior Vice President, Business Development and Film Finance	Gavin Levinson
Vice President, Accounting and Controller	Shannon Huntington
Manager, Accounts Payable	Sari Serber
Manager, Accounting	Grace D'Amico
Assistant to Jonathan Kier	Max Kondziolka
Assistant to Jenia Gorton	Liliana Granados

Business and Legal Affairs Executives, Development and Production	David Boyle
	Masha Koltsov Adam Macy Julianne Patterson

FOR eONE FEATURES

Executive Vice President, Production and Acquisitions	Lara Thompson
Executive Vice President, Content Strategy and Operations	Heidi Scheeline
Executive Vice President, Business and Legal Affairs	Michal Podell Steinberg
Vice President, Business and Legal Affairs	Rosalind Read
Production Consultant	Kate Fasulo
Senior Vice President, Finance	Monique Jones
Vice President, Finance	Evelyn Labonte
Vice President, Development	Ilda Diffley
Coordinator, Development	Aladdin El-Kadi

CALIFORNIA UNIT

Director of Photography	Andrew Davis
Production Designer	Victor Capoccia
First Assistant Photographer	Ryan Guzdziial
Second Assistant Photographer	Jay Stamm
Digital Imaging Technician	Mike Tarronas
Chief Lighting Technician	Scotty Frazer
Assistant Chief Lighting Technicians	Dessie Coale
	Steve Martinez
Electrician	Max Ciesynski
First Company Grip	Lucas Staley

Second Company Grip	Justin Bernard
Grip	Ruben Díaz
Location Manager	Travis Swantner
Property Master	Anthony Eikner
Costumer	Arieana Tate
Makeup Artist	Kelsey Berk
Makeup Effects Artist	Tanner White
Assistant Makeup Effects Artist	Patricia Heal
Hairstylist	D'nelle Almanza
Art Department Production Assistants	Madeline Jacobs
	Samuel Su
Production Assistants	Sarah Alvarez
	Limayri Fuentes
	Dustin Godwin

Visual Effects Provided by
VAN DYKE VISUAL EFFECTS

Visual Effects Supervisor	David Van Dyke
Visual Effects Producer	Shane Strickman
Compositing Supervisor	Matthew T. Wilson
Compositors	Kevin Shimamoto
	Jorge Zavala
Visual Effects Editor	George Woolley

Visual Effects Provided by
OUTPOST VFX

Visual Effects Supervisor	Marcin Kolendo
Visual Effects Producer	Geraint Hixson
Central Production Manager	Alysia Wildman
Visual Effects Artists	Ian Fellows
	Estevez Santos Elena
	Josh James Chappell
	Tom Rowell
Production Assistant	Remy Brown

Visual Effects Provided by
EYE SPY

Visual Effects Supervisor   Jose Marra

Digital Intermediate Provided by
ROUNDABOUT ENTERTAINMENT

Digital Colorist   Gregg Garvin
Digital Conform Editor   Vahe Giragol
Digital Intermediate Producer Carl Moore
Digital Cinema   Emmanuel Acosta
Data Management   Rene Clark
                                             Jose Castro
Account Executive   Jeannette Zepeda

Main Title Design by   Russell Andrew
End Titles Created with   Endcrawl®

Music Supervisor   Sean Mulligan
Music Coordinator   Victoria Beard

Songs

"OPEN HEART (FEAT. LISSIE)"
Written by Elisabeth Maurus and Morgan Page
Performed by Morgan Page and Lissie
Courtesy of Nettwerk Music Group Inc.

"POP GOES THE WEASEL"
Traditional

"NOT AS IT SEEMS"
Written and performed by Kevin MacLeod
Licensed under Creative Commons: By Attribution 3.0
Courtesy of Incompetech

"DRAGULA"
Written by Rob Zombie and Scott Humphrey
Performed by Lissie

Rights and Clearances by	Entertainment Clearances, Inc.
	Cassandra Barbour
	Meagan Sevier
Production Financing by	City National Bank, N.A.
	David Acosta
Legal Counsel to City National Bank, N.A.	Babok & Robinson, LLP
Completion Guarantor	Film Finances
Production Incentive Administration Provided by	EP Financial Solutions
Payroll Services by	Greenslate
Drone Photography by	Skylark Aerials Cincinnati
	Charles Detzel
	Trent Pekkala
	Robert Gerding
Mural Courtesy of	Artworks
Stock Footage Provided by	Shutterstock

The Filmmakers Wish to Thank
CAL POLY PUBLIC SAFETY
THE BECK FAMILY
CHRISTY BECK
ANTHONY BURGIO
DANIEL COHAN
RYAN CUNNINGHAM
JULIA GLAUSI
MICHAEL LUEHRSEN
AUSTIN LYON
KURT OBERHAUS

ALYSSA ROEHRENBECK
TRAVIS SHEPHERD
SHANE SIMMONS
HAMZA TALHOUNI
COREY WALLACE
THE WOODS AND READING FAMILY
LT. PAUL KUNKEL AND
THE NEWPORT, KY POLICE DEPARTMENT

PRODUCTION MATERIALS

HAUNT
DANGER HOUSE PRODUCTIONS, LLC

DIRECTOR	Scott Beck, Bryan Woods
PRODUCERS:	Mark Fasano, Todd Garner, Ankur Rungta
	Vishal Rungta, Eli Roth
EXEC. PRODUCERS:	Marc Schaberg, Josie Lang
	Tobial Weymar, Sean Robins
LINE PRODUCER/ UPM:	Jon D. Wagner

ALL PRE CALLS MUST ND8/ NO FORCED CALLS WITHOUT PRIOR APPROVAL FROM THE UPM.

*** NO PERSONAL PHOTOGRAPHY OR POSTING*** /CLOSED SET, ANY VISITORS MUST BE PRE-APPROVED BY UPM

Courtesy Crew Breakfast rts @10:15am(@Basecamp)

NEAREST HOSPITAL:				
ST. ELIZABETH COVINGTON	**CREW CALL**	**SHOOTING CALL**	**Sunrise: 8:05am Sunset: 6:37pm**	
COVINGTON, KY 41011			**Weather:**	Hi: 48° Lo: 34°
Current Script: PINK 10/17/17	**11:00am**	**12:00pm**	Sunny	
Current Schedule: PINK 10/19/17			10%	
			Tami Kumin- Key 2nd AD	

TRAUTH- 1ST FLOOR

SCENES	SET	CAST	DAY	PAGES	NOTES	LOCATION
A33	INT. MAZE > TUNNEL- EXIT	1, 4	N1	1/8		SET: TRAUTH/ 1st FLOOR
	HARPER & EVAN QUICKLY SQUEEZE OUT OF TUNNER, MALLORY NOT WITH THEM					
34	INT. MAZE > TUNNEL EXIT	1, 4, 12	N1	1 4/8	DEVIL MASK	
	HARPER, EVAN, YELL FOR MALLORY. DEVIL APPEARS AND POINTS TO YELLOW DOOR					
48	INT. MAZE > TUNNEL EXIT	1, 2, 3, 4, 5, 8	N1	4 5/8	ANGELA-BRUISED HAND GHOST MASK	
	THERE'S A CEMENT WALL BEHIND THE EXIT DOOR. EVAN PLANS HOW THEY'LL GET OUT					
50	INT. MAZE > TUNNEL EXIT	1, 2, 3, 5, 8	N1	4/8	ANGELA-BRUISED HAND GHOST MASK	
	THE GROUP WAITS FOR EVANS SIGNAL, HEARS A NOISE, HARPER LOCKS YELLOW DOOR					
53	INT. MAZE > TUNNEL EXIT	1, 2, 3, 5, 8	N1	2/8	ANGELA-BRUISED HAND GHOST MASK	**WORK TRUCK STAGING:**
	NATHAN USES IRON ROD TO PROMPT GHOST TO ENTER TUNNEL					**TRAUTH PARKING LOT-**
57	INT. MAZE > TUNNEL EXIT	1, 2, 3, 5	N1	2/8	ANGELA-BRUISED HAND	**PARK AS DIRECTED**
	NATHAN PACES NERVOUSLY, WONDERING WHAT'S TAKING SO LONG					**BASECAMP/ CATERING**
59	INT. MAZE > TUNNEL EXIT	1, 2, 3, 5	N1	2/8	ANGELA-BRUISED HAND	
	NATHAN ENTERS THE TUNNEL, HARPER STILL LISTENS AT YELLOW DOOR					
				TOTAL 7 4/8		

ID #	CAST	CHARACTER	SWF	LEAVE @	H/MU/W	SET CALL	REMARKS
1	KATIE STEVENS	HARPER	W	10:12AM	10:30AM	11:30AM	REPORT TO BASECAMP
2	WILL BRITTAIN	NATHAN	W	12:42PM	1:00PM	1:30PM	REPORT TO BASECAMP
3	LAURYN McCLAIN	BAILEY	W	11:42AM	12:00PM	1:30PM	REPORT TO BASECAMP
4	ANDREW CALDWELL	EVAN	W	10:42AM	11:00AM	11:30AM	REPORT TO BASECAMP
5	SHAZI RAJA	ANGELA	W	11:42AM	12:00PM	1:30PM	REPORT TO BASECAMP
6	SCHUYLER HELFORD	MALLORY	H	-	-	-	HOLD
8	CHANEY MORROW	GHOST	W	-	1:00PM	1:30PM	REPORT TO BASECAMP
12	DAMIAN MAFFEI	DEVIL	SW	-	10:45AM	11:30AM	REPORT TO BASECAMP

STAND-INS	CALL TIME	SET CALL	ATMOSPHERE CON'T			CALL TIME	SET CALL
HARPER UTILITY STAND IN	11:00AM	11:00AM					
EVAN UTILITY STAND IN	11:00AM	11:00AM					
GHOST/ DEVIL UTILITY STAND IN	11:00AM	11:00AM					
NATHAN UTILITY STAND IN	1:30PM	1:30PM					
BAILEY UTILITY STAND IN	1:30PM	1:30PM					
ANGELA UTILITY STAND IN	1:30PM	1:30PM					

*****SPECIAL INSTRUCTIONS *****   ******PLEASE CONSULT YOUR PERSONAL BREAKDOWN TO ENSURE ACCURACY******

PROPS: SC. 48- IRON ROD/ SC. 50- GHOST KEYS/ SC. 52- HOT FIRE POKER, IRON ROD/ SC. 59- GHOST'S KEYS, IRON ROD

WARDROBE: DEVIL- BLACK ROBE

SFX TOLIN: ATMOSPHERE SMOKE

MASKS: GHOST & DEVIL

MAKE-UP- BRUISED HAND FOR ANGELA

ADVANCED SCHEDULE -WED, NOV. 1, 2017 - APPROX CALL TIME: 12:00PM

SCENES	SET	CAST	DAY	PAGES	NOTES	LOCATION
	TRAUTH- 1ST FLOOR					
64	INT. MAZE > TUNNEL EXIT	1, 3 ,5	N1	2/8		SET: TRAUTH/ 1st FLOOR
	HARPER HEARS THE FOOTSTEPS STOP RIGHT OUTSIDE YELLOW DOOR, THE KNOB TURNS					
68	INT. MAZE > TUNNEL EXIT	1, 3, 5, 12, 100, 105	N1	1 1/8	ANGELA GETS STABBED DEVIL MASK	
	DEVIL PUSHES THRU DOOR, PULLS ANGELA OUT OF TUNNEL, STABS HER WITH PITCHFORK					
	SLIDE/GRAVEYARD					
35	INT. SLIDE	1, 4, 12	N1	7/8		
	CHAINSAW WAS SPEAKERS. HEAR REAL CHAINSAWS BELOW. THEY GO DOWN SLIDE					
36	INT. GRAVEYARD	1, 4, 13, 100, 113	N1	1 7/8	ZOMBIE MASK	
	ZOMBIE SCARES EVAN & HARPER WITH CHAIN-LESS SAW; THEY SINK INTO QUICKSAND					
47	INT. GRAVEYARD	1, 2, 3, 4, 5, 8	N1	3/8		**WORK TRUCK STAGING:**
	THE GROUP BACKTRACKS TO THE EXIT. EVAN HELPS THEM AVOID QUICKSAND					**TRAUTH PARKING LOT-**
69	INT. GRAVEYARD	1, 12	N1	2/8	DEVIL MASK	**PARK AS DIRECTED**
	HARPER EXITS THE SLIDE, DEVIL CHASES HER					**BASECAMP/ CATERING**
				TOTAL 4 6/8		

ADVANCED SCHEDULE - THURS NOV 2, 2017 - APPROX. CALL TIME 12:00PM

SCENES	SET	CAST	DAY	PAGES	NOTES	LOCATION
	TRAUTH- 1ST FLOOR					
49	INT. TUNNEL	4	N1	1/8		SET: TRAUTH/ 1st FLOOR
	EVAN CRAWLS THRU DARK TUNNEL					
51	INT. TUNNEL	4	N1	1/8		
	EVAN SEES LIGHTS UP AHEAD					
55	INT. TUNNEL	8	N1	1/8	GHOST MASK	
	THE GHOST SEES LIGHTS UP AHEAD					
61	INT. TUNNEL	2	N1	2/8		
	NATHAN STRUGGLES THROUGH THE TUNNEL, HEARS A THUMPING NOISE					
65	INT. TUNNEL	2	N1	1/8		**WORK TRUCK STAGING:**
	NATHAN HITS ANOTHER DEAD END, POUNDS WALL IN FRUSTRATION					**TRAUTH PARKING LOT-**
71	INT. TUNNEL	2, 3	N1	5/8		**PARK AS DIRECTED**
	NATHAN CALLS TO BAILEY IN THE DARK, TRAP-DOOR SOUND, NATHAN IS GONE					**BASECAMP/ CATERING**
32	INT. MAZE > TUNNEL	1, 4, 6	N1	1 2/8		
	EVAN, HARPER, MALLORY MANEUVER THRU TUNNEL, HEAR A LOUD CRACK					
	DUNGEON					
26	INT. HAUNTED HOUSE, DUNGEON	1, 2, 3, 4, 5, 6, 18, 100, 110	N1	1 2/8		
	GROUP WATCHES WITCH PUSH RED HOT ROD INTO GIRL'S FACE, HER FACE MELTS					
				TOTAL 3 7/8		

UPM	**1st A.D.:**	**Key 2nd A.D:**
Jon D. Wagner	Doug Turner	Tami Kumin

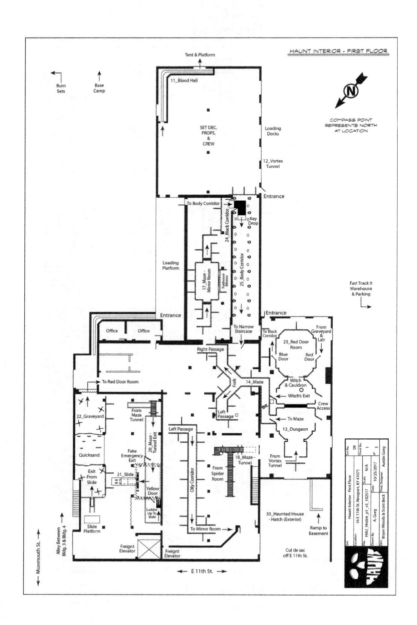

HAUNT INTERIOR - FIRST FLOOR

Tent & Platform

11_Blood Hall

SET DEC,
PROPS,
&
CREW

Loading
Docks

12_Vortex
Tunnel

Entrance

To Body Corridor

Key
Drop

Loading
Platform

17_Maze -
Mirror Room

24_Black Corridor

25_Body Corridor

Entrance

Entrance

To Narrow
Staircase

To Black
Corridor

From
Graveyard
& Lab

23_Red Door
Room

Office   Office

Right Passage

Blue
Door

Red
Door

To Red Door Room

Fork

14_Maze

Witch
& Cauldron

Witch's Exit

Crew
Access

Left
Passage

22_Graveyard

From
Maze
Tunnel

20_Maze -
Tunnel Exit

Left Passage

To Maze

13_Dungeon

Quicksand

Fake
Emergency
Exit

18_Maze -
Tunnel

From
Spider
Room

From
Vortex
Tunnel

Exit
From
Slide

21_Slide

Yellow
Door

Olly Corridor

Slide
Platform

Ladder
Up To
Slide

To Mirror Room

33_Haunted House
- Hatch (Exterior)

Freight
Elevator

Freight
Elevator

Ramp to
Basement

E 11th St.

Cul de sac
off E 11th St.

Monmouth St.

Alley Between
Bldg. 3 & Bldg. 4

Burn
Sets

Base
Camp

COMPASS POINT
REPRESENTS NORTH
AT LOCATION

Fast Track It
Warehouse
& Parking

Haunt Interior - First Floor
16 E 11th St, Newport, KY 41071
HAU_Hrdint_p1_v1_H0517
N/A
10/25/2017
A. Gong
Austin Gong
Bryan Woods & Scott Beck
09
1
of 3

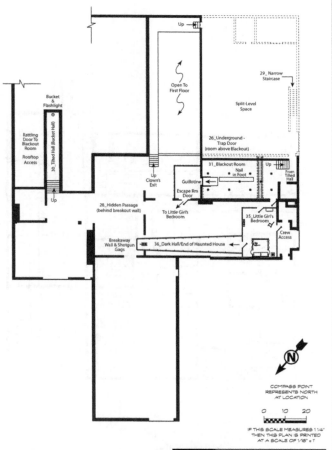

Up

29_ Narrow
Staircase

Open To
First Floor

Split-Level
Space

Bucket
&
Flashlight

26_Underground -
Trap Door
(room above Blackout)

Rattling
Door To
Blackout
Room

31_Blackout Room

Nail
in Foot

Up

From
Tilted
Hall

Rooftop
Access

Up
Clown's
Exit

Guillotine

Escape Rm
Door

28_Hidden Passage
(behind breakout wall)

To Little Girl's
Bedroom

35_Little Girl's
Bedroom

Crew
Access

Breakaway
Wall & Shotgun
Gags

36_Dark Hall/End of Haunted House

Up

N

COMPASS POINT
REPRESENTS NORTH
AT LOCATION

0   10   20

IF THIS SCALE MEASURES 1 1/4"
THEN THIS PLAN IS PRINTED
AT A SCALE OF 1/16" = 1'

Set:	Haunt Interior - Second Floor		Set No. 09
Location:			Sheet No.
Title: HAU_HntInt_p2_v3_102517		Scale: 1/16" = 1'	2
Drawn By: A. Gorg		Date: 10/25/2017	of 3
Writer: Bryan Woods & Scott Beck		Prod. Designer: Austin Gorg	

HAUNT

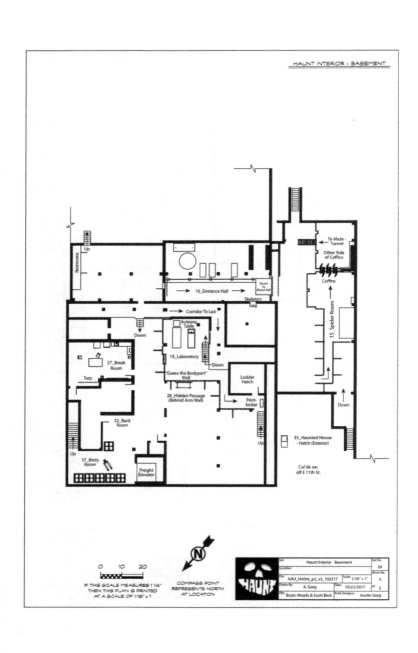

To Maze - Tunnel

Other Side of Coffins

Coffins

15_Spider Room

Restrooms

Up

Down to Blood Hall

10_Entrance Hall

Skeleton Gag

Corridor To Lab

Autopsy Table

Down

19_Laboratory

Down

"Guess the Bodypart" Wall

Ladder Hatch

27_Break Room

Tarp

28_Hidden Passage (Behind Arm Wall)

Foot-locker

32_Back Room

Down

33_Haunted House - Hatch (Exterior)

Up

Up

37_Body Room

Freight Elevator

Cul de sac off E 11th St.

0   10   20

IF THIS SCALE MEASURES 1 1/4" THEN THIS PLAN IS PRINTED AT A SCALE OF 1/16" = 1'

N

COMPASS POINT REPRESENTS NORTH AT LOCATION

HAUNT

Site:	Haunt Interior - Basement	Set No. 09
Location:		Sheet No.
File: HAU_HntInt_p3_v3_102517	Scale: 1/16" = 1'	3
Drawn By: A. Gorg	Date: 10/25/2017	of 3
Dir: Bryan Woods & Scott Beck	Prod. Design: Austin Gorg	

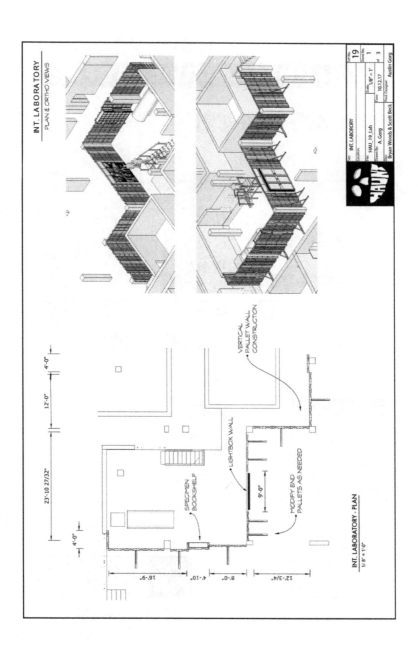

INT. LABORATORY
PLAN & ORTHO VIEWS

VERTICAL
PALLET WALL
CONSTRUCTION

LIGHTBOX WALL

SPECIMEN
BOOKSHELF

MODIFY END
PALLETS AS NEEDED

9'-0"

4'-0"
12'-0"
23'-10 27/32"
4'-0"

16'-9"
4'-10"
8'-0"
12'-3/4"

INT. LABORATORY - PLAN
1/8" = 1'-0"

INT. LABORATORY
Location:
File: HAU_19_Lab
Drawn By: A. Gorg
Date: 10.12.17
Scale: 1/8" = 1'
Lead Designer: Austin Gorg
Design: Bryan Woods & Scott Beck

Set No. 19
Sheet No. 1
of 3

HAUNTED FLOWCHART

BACK ROOM

BODY ROOM

BLACK CORRIDOR

SUFFOCATION TUNNEL

BODY CORRIDOR

NARROW STAIRCASE

UNDRGRND - TRAPDOOR

TILTED HALL

OTHER SIDE COFFINS

MAZE - TUNNEL

MAZE - TUNNEL EXIT

SLIDE

BLACKOUT ROOM

SPIDER ROOM

RED DOOR ROOM

GRAVEYARD

LITTLE GIRLS ROOM

MAZE FORK

MAZE ENTRANCE

DARK HALL

DUNGEON

MAZE - L PASSAGE

MIRROR ROOM

LABORATORY

END OF HAUNT

BEHIND MIRROR

VORTEX TUNNEL

HIDDEN PASSAGE

HIDDEN PASS - HATCH

HIDDEN PASS - WALL

MAZE - L PASSAGE

BURN SET - LOCATION TBD

BLOOD HALL

BREAK ROOM

HAUNT - HATCH

ENTRANCE HALL

EXT HAUNTED HOUSE

PARKING LOT

PERIMETER FENCE

HAUNTED LEGEND

PLAYERS	PORTENTS
Harper	Death
Nathan	Fire
Bailey	
Evan	
Mallory	
Angela	
Nameless Victim	
Devil	
Clown	
Witch	
Zombie	
Ghost	
Vampire	
Grim Reaper (Bailey)	

Set:	Haunted House Geography Flowchart	Set No. N/A
Location:	Trauth (Int) & Jolly (Ext)	Sheet No. 1
File: HAU_GeoChrt_v1_092017	Scale: N/A	
Drawn By: A. Gorg	Date: 09/20/2017	of 1
Dir: Bryan Woods & Scott Beck	Prod. Designer: Austin Gorg	

HAUNT

52   INT. MAZE > ~~BACKOF~~ SPIDER ROOM - NIGHT   52

Evan squeezes out of the tunnel. He SLAPS the wall three
times and yells:

                    EVAN
          I'm through!

53   INT. MAZE > TUNNEL EXIT - NIGHT

Nathan stands with the ROD aimed at the GHOST.

                    NATHAN
          You're up.

The GHOST crawls into the tunnel.

54   INT. MAZE - NIGHT   54

Evan runs through the maze.

Everything looks different on the way back.

Completely different.

Did he miss a turn?

55   INT. TUNNEL - NIGHT   55

The GHOST sees light up ahead.

56   INT. MAZE > ~~BACKOF~~ SPIDER ROOM - NIGHT   56

The GHOST slinks out of the tunnel. Stands. Looks around the
room. Spiderwebs matted down from where Evan ran through.

57   INT. MAZE > TUNNEL EXIT - NIGHT   57

Nathan paces nervously.

                    NATHAN
          What's taking so long.

58   INT. MAZE > ~~BACKOF~~ SPIDER ROOM - NIGHT   58

The GHOST stares at the far wall.

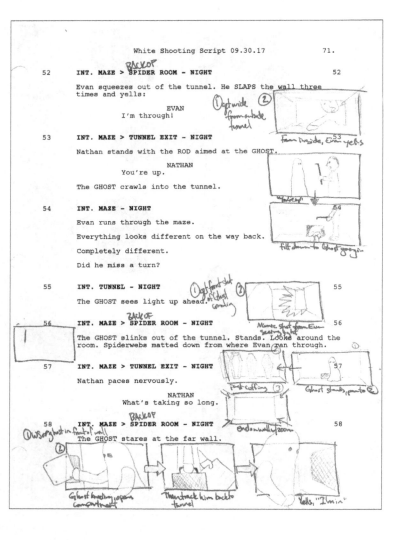

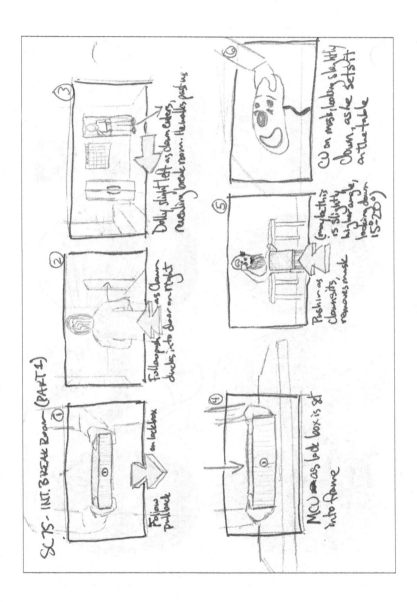

SC 75 - INT. BREAK Room (PART 1)

① Fabian pullback on lockbox

② Follow Ralph as Clown ducks into door on right

③ Dolly slight left as Clown exits, revealing break room. He walks past us

④ MCU as locked box is set into frame

⑤ Push in as Clown sits, removes mask (angle this is slightly high angle, looking down 15-20°)

⑥ CU on mask looking slightly Clown, as he sets it on the table

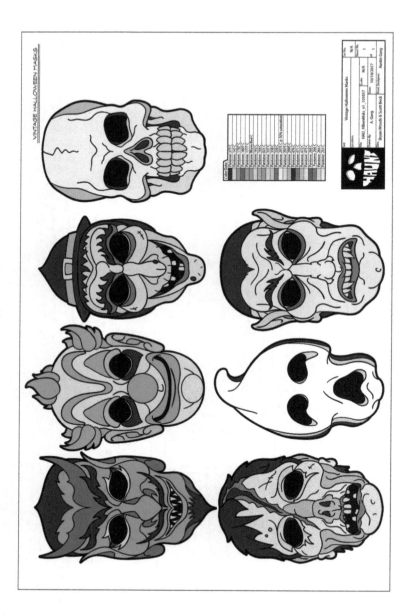

ABOUT THE WRITERS

Filmmakers Scott Beck & Bryan Woods burst onto the Hollywood scene with Paramount Pictures' *A Quiet Place*, based on their original screenplay. The critically acclaimed box-office smash stars Emily Blunt alongside John Krasinski, who also directed. The film earned over $340 million at the worldwide box-office and was #1 at the domestic box-office for two weeks. Beck & Woods serve as Executive Producers on the film in addition to co-writing the screenplay.

A Quiet Place was named as a Top Ten Film of 2018 by the American Film Institute and the National Board of Review. Beck & Woods' script earned them the Saturn Award for Best Writing, alongside nominations from the Writers Guild and the Critics Choice Awards, and was named one of the year's ten best scripts by The Tracking Board Hit List. Variety went on to name Beck & Woods to their annual 10 Screenwriters to Watch list.

Next up for Beck & Woods is Sony Pictures' sci-fi thriller *65* with Academy Award® nominee Adam Driver starring along with Ariana Greenblatt and Chloe Coleman. The film is an original screenplay written by the duo, which they also serve as directors and producers under their Beck/Woods banner alongside producer Sam Raimi.

Also on deck for the duo is *The Boogeyman*, based on Stephen King's iconic short story of the same name. They wrote the screenplay and serve as Executive Producers on the film. The short story, first published in 1973 and later released in King's 1978 collection *Night Shift*, followed a man who's recently lost all his children to a creature lurking in the closet. King himself gave his endorsement of *A Quiet Place*, tweeting that the film "is an extraordinary piece of work."

Other credits for the filmmakers include 2019's acclaimed thriller *Haunt*, which they wrote and directed for producer Eli Roth, Sierra/Affinity, Broken Road Productions, and Nickel City Pictures.

Beck & Woods are members of the Directors Guild of America and the Writers Guild of America.